THE
CANNING, FREEZING, CURING & SMOKING
OF MEAT, FISH & GAME

Wilbur F. Eastman, Jr.

Illustrations by Douglas Merrilees

A Garden Way Publishing Book

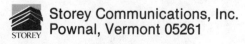

Storey Communications, Inc.
Pownal, Vermont 05261

To MCE with love

To Mary and Dave Eybers
Who first shared with me the joys
of smoking —
With hickory, that is!

The publisher wishes to thank Lavon L. Bartel, Ph.D., R.D., of the
University of Vermont Extension Service for help with updating and
revising this book in 1989.

Printed in the United States by Capital City Press
Fifteenth printing, May 1991

Library of Congress Catalog Card Number: 75-16830
International Standard Book Number: 0-88266-045-4

CONTENTS

1 Some Basic Information   1
2 Canning   11
3 Freezing   39
4 Curing   53
5 How to Build a Smokehouse and Do It Yourself   73
6 Beef and Veal   83
7 Pork   101
8 Lamb   119
9 Poultry   125
10 Game   137
11 Fish   147
12 Recipes   167
   Index   197

INTRODUCTION

This book has been designed to provide basic and safe information to help the home owner process meat, fish and game.

By processing is meant the procedures for canning, freezing, curing, and smoking; in other words storing meat for future use.

Even if you should decide not to do your own processing, the book can still provide you with an understanding of what has happened to the meat products you see in the markets and which you may ultimately purchase for household needs.

It is purposely intended that the reader will find a certain amount of repetition in the book, not only concerning preparation and processing but also concerning the precautions one must take to achieve these activities safely. Since this is basically a **do-it-yourself reference book,** the reader is not expected to read the entire book each time he wants directions; instead he will refer to the process he intends to use or to the type of meat he wishes to process. To save his time and to make the book as efficient and practical a tool as possible, some amount of repetition and referral seemed not only reasonable but also important.

Nor can any book of this sort presume to be complete. The reader therefore is frequently referred to the instructions the manufacturer supplies with processing equipment, and he is alerted to the fact that new materials and equipment are constantly coming on to the market.

The recipe section (Chapter 12) contains certain selected recipes that should show the reader that processing is simple and may be made personal; it is by no means meant to be a complete round-up of processed meats, but it is meant to encourage the reader to strike out on his own providing he does not disregard the customary precautions that have been discussed. With the many, many books on the market containing an endless number of recipes for hams, sausages, and other processed meats, there is little reason to try to duplicate them here.

When researching material for a book, the author frequently encounters a variety of methods and directions in connection with various facets of the subject under investigation. Sometimes these methods and directions are at considerable variance with one another. The subject of processing meat is no exception to this experience.

For instance, there are honest debates concerning the value of saltpeter for curing meat. Some insist it controls botulism; some insist with equal fervor that any such control is slight if indeed it exists at all. Others maintain its main purpose is to give meat a bright color; still others maintain that saltpeter is an additive that could possibly be harmful to the body, that meat can just as easily be cured without it, and that there are other ways to protect against botulism.

Another such area of sharp differences is home processing vs. commercial processing. Certainly commercial plants, especially those under rigid federal control and inspection, are required to butcher, chill, and process within fine temperature ranges with specific and definite standards for brines and precise periods for the smoking process.

Since this book is concerned with home processing, we cannot insist that the reader use the same controlled conditions he would find in a commercial packing house, nor can we expect that he can use the identical methods for processing meat. Such exact and well respected conditions cannot be achieved on the farm with the controls a commercial plant is equipped to handle. Therefore we have tried wherever possible to present a standard that has been established for home and farm use, one that is safe to follow. For this standard and to make the book as authoritative as possible, we have relied heavily on publications of the United States Department of Agriculture, the United States Department of the Interior, the Canada Department of Agriculture in Ottawa, various state universities, and publications of certain manufacturers of processing supplies and equipment.

Acknowledgments

To the United States Department of Agriculture, the United States Department of the Interior and especially its Fish and Wildlife Service, and the Canada Department of Agriculture in Ottawa for their many helpful bulletins and publications I am indeed grateful. Various state universities have also provided me with helpful publications, some of which were research reports undertaken jointly with the United States Department of Agriculture, and they have my sincere thanks. And to the manufacturers of processing equipment who provided me with their publications, I am most grateful.

All photographs have been taken by **John Guion Perry** expressly for this book; the original artwork was prepared by **Douglas Merrilees;** and their work on the book's behalf is recognized and acknowledged with gratitude.

I am especially indebted to the following individuals for their suggestions and help and for some of the recipes in Chapter 12: **Janet Anderson; Mrs. Elizabeth Brouha; Mother and Dad Eastman; Mary and Dave Eybers; Mrs. Helen Gilmore; Michael Hotaling; Carl Koenig; Mrs. Alice Rowe;** and **Henry Wagner** for all sorts of helpful information in his meat classes. **Glenn Anderson** of Morton Salt Company and another reader who has wished to remain anonymous read and re-read the manuscript and made very helpful suggestions, many of which were incorporated into the manuscript; for such assistance I am indeed indebted to them.

And to my editor, Edward Miller, I say thanks for the many things, all too numerous to mention, that made for improving the book.

Wilbur F. Eastman, Jr.
The Lodge
Groton, Vermont
September, 1975

1
SOME BASIC INFORMATION

PROCESSING

Seldom does a family want to consume an entire beef as soon as it is slaughtered or an entire hog or wild deer. Not only would this cause the animal to lose its welcome, but it would not allow some of the beef and pork to be consumed later when market prices are higher, venison to be eaten throughout the year, or having meat available for a balanced diet. Neither would it allow for the enjoyment of the succulent ham, corned beef, bacon, and smoked tongue that are high on the list of choice meats of most families; for it takes time to make these choice meats.

Spreading the availability of meat out over future months and to provide for a balanced diet require that it be preserved, or stored, in some manner until it is wanted for the table. But to store meat requires that the growth of enzymes in it that cause negative food action must be halted, and that harmful microorganisms be at least put into a dormant stage, if not killed altogether.

It is easy to impede the growth of enzymes and of negative organisms and to kill them outright in some instances so meat may be preserved, or stored, for future use without its deterioration and spoilage. This is done in several ways: canning, freezing, curing, and smoking. It is also accomplished when meat is dried, and when fat is rendered into lard. We call this processing.

This book, then, is concerned with ways of processing meat; and when we say meat, we include poultry, fish, and game. The emphasis is on canning, freezing, curing and smoking, but we shall mention some of the other ways meat and meat products are processed for storage until wanted for later use.

When we discuss processing methods in future chapters, you will be advised to can meat at 240° F, to freeze meat at -10° F or below, and to take precautions in curing to be certain that salt penetrates deep into meat to withdraw moisture and to make it uninhabitable for bacteria and other microorganisms to thrive. And over and over we shall remind you to take careful sanitary precautions when handling meat.

Why?

To understand why, we need some background information on enzymes and microorganisms.

ENZYMES AND MICROORGANISMS

Enzymes

These are natural substances formed in plant and animal cells. They cause fermentation and break down tissues in the meat by working on the proteins, fats, and carbohydrates. When meat is being chilled, their catalytic action tenderizes meat; however when meat is canned, unless their action is stopped by heat, unpleasant changes in color, texture, and flavor will occur. A temperature of approximately 150°F will destroy most enzyme action; but to kill certain microorganisms, we shall need a much higher temperature (240°F); so the 240°F temperature will do both favors for us at the same time.

Negative enzyme action is also greatly slowed down by cold; so when we hold frozen meat at 0° F, we may be sure that negative enzyme action has been reduced below the danger point. Fish must be kept at -10°F. or below.

Microorganisms

There are three types of microorganisms that we are concerned with: molds, yeasts, and bacteria. They are found everywhere -- in air, in water, and in the ground. But let's take them one at a time.

1 **Molds.** Molds are a downy or furry growth. They are caused by fungi and are found on the surface of organic matter, especially where there is dampness and decay. Boiling heat will destroy molds, and they will become inactive in temperatures under 32°F.

2 **Yeasts.** These are also fungi causing fermentation and consequent food spoilage. They are inactive at 0°F and below, but a temperature of 240°F will assure that they are long since dead.

3 **Bacteria.** There are many kinds of bacteria—good ones and bad ones — but we must guard against the kind that spoil meat. This means we must destroy them to prevent their spreading, for they will continue to grow in canned food unless destroyed during processing. Soft, slimy, and flat sour food is evidence of their negative action. Growth of bacteria ceases below 32°F, and most bacteria cells are killed at 190°F; however their spores (seeds) may continue to live on at this temperature but are destroyed at a temperature of 240°F. Bacteria are the most stubborn of the microorganisms to destroy, and the most deadly of the bacteria is the one causing botulism.

    Botulism is caused by a toxin (poisonous compound) made in sealed containers of food by the spores of a particular bacteria called <u>clostridium botulinum</u>. They have the ability to grow in moist foods when oxygen is not present. Their growth cells are inactive at freezing temperatures, but it requires a higher temperature (190°F) to destroy the cells. Their spores require an even higher temperature of 240°F to be destroyed.

The botulism toxin is deadly in most instances, and to be on the safe side, all canned food should be boiled for twenty minutes in an open saucepan; if there is any toxin present due to an error in processing, it will be killed. Furthermore, if the canned food has spoiled, a bad odor from the saucepan may alert you to spoilage, in which case DESTROY THE FOOD WITHOUT EVEN TASTING and sterilize the saucepan. Note, however, that botulinum does not necessarily cause a bad odor.

Federal Meat Inspection

The United States Government has set up standards of sanitation for establishments slaughtering and processing meat products. No doubt you have noticed a stamp on fresh meat similar to Figure 1-1 below; this means that it has been inspected for wholesomeness and freedom from disease; and that the establishment where the animal was slaughtered and processed was inspected by federal inspectors to meet the federal standards.

U.S. Inspection Stamp for Fresh & Cured Meats.
Figure 1-1

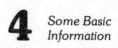

A stamp like Figure 1-2 is found on canned or packaged meat products that have been similarly inspected and approved for wholesomeness and freedom from disease. These standards are set up by the Department of Agriculture under whose jurisdiction the inspections are carried out.

U.S. Inspection Stamp for Canned & Packaged Meat Products.

Figure 1-2

In Canada the Dominion Department of Agriculture similarly sets standards for wholesomeness and for sanitation. Its stamp is similar to Figure 1-3.

Since these are federal and dominion stamps, they pertain only to those establishments that are involved with interstate (interprovincial) and foreign sales. They are not required for intrastate (intraprovincial) sale; standards for local use are set up by local governments.

Because these stamps attest to high standards of sanitation

Canadian Inspection Stamp.
Figure 1-3

and wholesomeness, we advise that anyone having a farm animal to slaughter would do well to inquire at a federally inspected slaughterhouse to determine if it performs what is called "custom slaughtering." Should this be the case, your animal will be inspected along with the other animals being slaughtered for its wholesomeness and freedom from disease, and you may be assured that it will be slaughtered with top sanitary conditions.

Grading Meat

Federal meat graders in the packing house -- those with expertise in knowing the quality of meat -- grade beef so the consumer will know how it should be valued when for sale in retail outlets. The grades -- Prime, Choice, Select, Commercial, or Utility -- are stamped on the meat; its grade being a consideration of the general physical shape of the animal carcass, the color and distribution of fat, and the amount of marbelized fat and texture of the meat.

Prime is the highest in quality. Choice is also of excellent quality but with less fat marbelized throughout than prime. Select is still fine quality but with very little fat, and Commercial is less tender and most likely from older animals. The grade marked "Utility" is lacking in juices and tender quality, has practically no fat, and is apt to be from even older animals.

Figure 1-4 illustrates the markings of the federal graders.

USDA Grading Stamps for Beef.
Figure 1-4

Beef is the only type of meat graded for retail sale as a common thing, but others are graded on an optional basis or upon special request.

In Canada beef is the only type of meat graded for retail sale, and only two grades are noted: Choice and Good. Choice is indicated by a red-colored stripe and Good by a blue one.

ALWAYS
PLAY IT SAFE

Throughout this book we shall emphasize playing it safe. One's health and one's safety are too valuable to take unnecessary risks. While processing one's own meat will assist very considerably in holding down the family food budget, there still is an investment in jars and equipment in addition to the meat; and unless one follows the tested methods of processing, one is courting loss and disaster. This is not to admit that some have been lucky while using unapproved methods, but there is no substitute for doing it right, especially when the right way costs no more and is safer.

The United States Government, as well as private industries, are constantly researching for new ways to help the consumer, and they test their methods for months and months under controlled conditions before issuing their findings for consumer use. Furthermore when they find it necessary to advocate discarding unapproved methods, you may assume it is for well established reasons.

So when we can meat and do not use an oven or microwave for canning, we are not saying that it has not been tried, and successfully; but we are saying that the risks involved in terms of personal safety and food safety are just too much; and both government and private industries that research canning methods all agree that the safest method, by far, for canning is the use of the pressure canner. We'll constantly remind you of things like this throughout the book because they are so important.

No one will disagree with the advice that the best way to have top quality processed products is to start with top quality meat. This does not mean that you must always purchase prime grade; choice may be quite adequate for your needs, but be sure that choice is top quality choice. And be certain that you keep its quality top quality by respecting the fundamentals of the processing method you use all the way from proper sanitation at the start right on down to storage.

New Methods and New Products on The Market

New methods and new materials for processing are constantly being researched and experimented with. Even pressure canners are not all alike because a certain manufacturer may find ways to make improvements on his particular model. We may expect an occasional new method or variation on a present one to be announced from time to time after adequate testing. New equipment and supplies are constantly being introduced to the market. In such cases, be sure to follow the instructions of the manufacturer and avoid trouble.

Sources of Information

Should any question arise about the advisability of using some particular piece of equipment or process, should you need information about proper timing, recipes for preparing different dishes, or just about anything concerning housekeeping, you have sources of information close to your fingertips.

The County Extension Agent is always as close as a phone call, and the office number may be found in your phone book, usually under state listings (or call Information). County Extension Agents are most helpful, and usually the answer can be given instantly. State universities are another source of information, especially in the College of Agriculture or Home Science. Manufacturers of supplies, for instance, of glass jars, are always helpful; and their addresses can usually be found on the jar carton; or ask your County Agent for them. State Fish and Game Commissions are sources of help and referral and frequently have useful publications of their own. And finally, government sources: the United States Department of Agriculture publishes pamphlets on a myriad of subjects concerning housekeeping and other subjects, specially written and illustrated for the consumer; write directly to the Publications Office, Department of Agriculture, Washington, D.C. 20250 or to the Government Printing Office, Washington, D.C. 20402 for the information you want. In Canada write to the Information Division, Department of Agriculture, Ottawa.

The Personal Touch

Even within the range of safe working, there is still a large area where one may experiment and specialize along lines of personal interest. Many people have become famous for their venison mincemeat, or for their corned beef, or for their home-smoked hams. They gained fame, not because they threw precautions to the wind and went their own ways, but because they followed instructions carefully to prevent food contamination; yet they worked up a special flavor combination that was strictly "theirs." They may have learned just how to brine corned beef with their own special mixture of ingredients until it was better than that of others, or until their experimentation found that a certain type of wood for smoking worked best with maple syrup as a sweetener in a ham pickle.

While we have tried to present a correct and safe way to process meat, the creative person will still find plenty of room to individualize his own products and gain some reputation within and beyond his own family for coming up with a product that is strictly his hallmark.

2
CANNING

WHY CAN MEATS, POULTRY, AND FISH?

Of the millions of families in the United States who can food each year, many can meat.* They do this for many reasons. What are these reasons?

1 **Canning is easy to do.** Learning to can is a simple procedure providing certain rules are followed without unapproved short-cuts. And the result is the availability of highly nutritious meats.

2 **It is economical to can.** The initial investment is small for containers and necessary utensils; furthermore most of the equipment may be re-used many times (except for the metal cans, rubber rings, and metal lids); so the investment may be spread over many years.

3 **Canning allows one to obtain and store in quantity** when meat is most easily available and when prices are lowest. This further adds to the economy of canning.

4 **Canned food is easy to keep** since containers are more or less standard in size and allow for convenient storing.

*All references to "meat(s)" in this chapter refer to poultry, fish, and game as well as to beef, pork, lamb, and veal; any exceptions will be specifically identified.

5   Except when using metal cans, **canned food is easy to see and identify.** But even with metal cans careful labeling will identify the contents.
6   Because cans and jars come in different sizes, the **contents provide convenient quantities** for use without having large amounts left over. And a sudden influx of company makes it simple to open a few cans or jars to provide for hungry appetites at a moment's notice.
7   While some people like to freeze meat, freezers are not available for everyone; so for them **canning meat is much more convenient.** Furthermore freezing meat has no advantages over canning insofar as preserving and edibility are concerned.
8   The process of canning, if done properly, will kill molds, yeasts, and bacteria which would otherwise contaminate food. Thus, spoilage is prevented.
9   Once meat is canned, there is no further cost (such as electricity if you freeze meat) to store the containers until their contents are consumed.

How To Select and Maintain Meat Preparatory to Canning

While special guidelines may be given in the separate chapters that include beef, pork, lamb, poultry, fish, and game, certain considerations that are of paramount importance when selecting and holding all kinds of meat to be canned follow:

1   Whether the animals are home-grown, obtained locally, or purchased from commercial outlets, be certain that the meat comes from a healthy animal.
    If purchased meat bears the approval stamps of federal or state inspectors, you have such assurance at the time you obtain it.

If there is any doubt whatsoever about home-grown or local meat, have it inspected by a veterinarian. In the case of wild game, a veterinarian should be asked to examine the carcass before any attempt is made to process the meat if there is the slightest doubt about its quality.

2 Until you are actually ready to can meat, it must be kept cool, and this means as close to 32° F as possible without freezing, but always well under 40° F. Why? To prevent spoilage, and incidently to increase its tenderness.

In the event there is no way to hold meat below 40° F and the air temperature is about 40° F, meat to be canned should be processed immediately after the animal's body temperature is gone.

If one plans ahead, one may be able to obtain meat for canning during the colder winter months when outside air temperature is frequently well under 40° F, making chilling easier.

3 If meat is to be held beyond a few days before being canned, it should be fast-frozen at -10° F and stored at 0° F, then thawed when ready to be canned. Such thawing should be done in a refrigerator at 40° F or lower until there are no longer signs of ice crystals on the meat.

What Does The Process of Canning Involve?

Canning is a method of storing food in air-tight containers in such a way that it is free from any danger of spoilage or contamination by bacteria, molds, and yeasts.

To accomplish this requires that the containers be sterilized; that all traces of bacteria, molds, and yeasts in the food be killed; and that all air be driven out of the food being canned. In order that canned food is not later contaminated by air from outside the containers, the containers must be sealed air-tight.

Heat, then, is required to kill all traces of bacteria, molds, and yeasts. This same heat is used to expel the air from the food and from the containers, which, together with normal shrinkage of the food during the canning process, creates a vacuum that seals the containers and prevents outside contamination.

Necessary Equipment

Pressure Canner

This is the one absolutely important piece of equipment you must have if you are going to can meat. In order that all bacteria spores may be killed without danger of food spoilage or contamination, the containers and food being canned must be heated to 240°F, which is impossible to do safely without building up 10-15 pounds of steam pressure, depending on altitude (see p. 16). And the only way to reach this temperature safely is with a pressure canner. Canning meat should never be attempted without one.

The importance of a pressure canner cannot be overemphasized. If you cannot find a pressure canner in good condition, forget about canning meat; think instead about other ways of processing it.

Pressure canners come in various sizes, and the right size for you will depend of course on how many there are in your household, how much canning you plan to do, the size of the containers you plan to use, and how and for what other purposes you plan to use your canner. A pressure canner may be used for

It has been pointed out that the standard kitchen pressure cooker used for cooking potatoes and vegetables for home consumption is capable of use as a pressure canner. Usually these pressure cookers do not have a gauge that registers the number of pounds of steam pressure or the interior temperature; thus they would be difficult to use for canning. Furthermore they would likely hold no more than three or four pint jars. So we do not recommend them. However if you wish to try your pressure cooker for canning instead of using a pressure canner, we would suggest that you check first with your County Extension Agent for any advice for your particular type of pressure cooker.

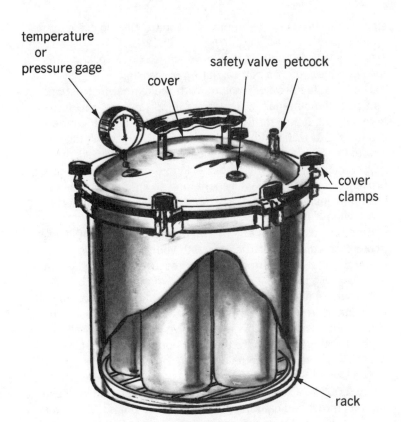

temperature
or
pressure gage

cover

safety valve petcock

cover
clamps

rack

Pressure Canner
Figure 2-1

many purposes other than for canning; it is terribly useful to
have around the kitchen for making stews, baking beans and
brown bread, cooking vegetables, and for countless other
purposes.

For a pressure canner to be in good working condition and
adequate for canning, it must have a cover that can be sealed
tight; a petcock to let out steam for about ten minutes at the
start of processing to be sure that all excess air is removed from
the inside of the canner; a temperature dial or pressure gauge to
record the inside temperature or pressure when steam is built
up; and a safety valve to let off excess steam in the event that

steam pressure is inadvertently allowed to build up close to the danger point.

Naturally the canner should have some sort of rack to keep the containers off the bottom during processing.

The manufacturer will include with the canner instructions on its use and maintenance. These are important, not only for your own safety but also for the proper processing of your canned products. Study these instructions carefully and don't take any shortcuts. A little extra time in cleaning out the petcock, in adjusting the rubber ring, and checking the thermometer or pressure gauge is time well spent, and so little in comparison with time lost if your food does not keep because of imperfect processing.

Since the containers of food will be processed at 240°F or above (according to instructions with your canner), it is important that the thermometer or pressure gauge be accurate. It is desirable to have it checked by the manufacturer or the outlet where it was purchased (see instructions that come with the canner) from time to time for this assurance. Or ask your County Extension Agent where to have it done. Never allow a pressure gauge to be more than five pounds off accurate pressure; if it is, you should discard it for a new one.

The United States Department of Agriculture advises that for every 2,000 feet you live above sea level you should increase the recommended canning pressure by one pound. With dial gauge canners, 11 lbs. pressure is required at 0-2000 feet, 12 lbs. at 2000-4000 feet, 13 lbs. at 4000-6000 feet, and 14 lbs. at 6000-8000 feet. Weighted pressure canners require 10 lbs. at 0-1000 feet, and 15 lbs. at altitudes greater than 1000 feet.

Sealer

A sealer is necessary if you plan to process your meat in metal cans. The manufacturer's instructions will tell you how to adjust the sealer to obtain a perfect seal. Even so, it is wise to test-seal a can by partly filling it with water, then dunking it completely in boiling water for a minute or slightly less. If air bubbles emerge from the can, you do not have a tight seal, and the sealer should be readjusted.

Jars and cans for containing food to be processed.
A discussion of this will be found on pages 23-30.

Thermometer
A rod-type thermometer will be necessary, especially if you choose the raw-pack method of canning, because meat will not be ready for the pressure canner until the contents of the containers reach 170°F. (Raw pack is not usually recommended for meats.)

Clock or other timer.
Much needed for accurate timing.

Can and jar lifter
Some sort of clamp or other gadget to lift metal cans and jars from the pressure canner at the end of the processing period will prevent burned fingers and protect the containers. There are several very efficient and inexpensive ones on the market.

Experience will show that there are a number of other utensils around the normal kitchen that will prove handy during canning: sauce pans, metal cups, and ladles, for instance. But the really important "must" ones are those listed above.

Precautions
The following precautions are just simple, common-sense ones, yet very important. They are the results of time-tested methods and experience of those in industry and government whose business it is to set standards for food safety. Treat these precautions with respect, and remember they are listed here only for the purpose of helping you to can food that will be both safe and nutritious for you and your family.

1 **Follow carefully the instructions** as to what cans, caps or lids to use. Read the instructions on the boxes. Likewise treat your pressure canner with respect and follow the instructions from the manufacturer as to its use and maintenance.
2 **Allow yourself no short-cuts.** Unless you have time to do it properly, you should forget completely

Using a Lifter for Moving Hot Jars and Cans

Figure 2-2

about canning. When packing metal cans and glass jars, leave the recommended headspace, process the containers the full amount of time recommended but no more. Don't allow yourself to be rushed.

3 **Follow instructions** that will be described later concerning the rapid cooling of canned meat and its proper storage.

4 **Maintain absolute cleanliness at all times.** Failure to do so can easily result in spoilage and food contamination, poor seals, and even illness. Not only should all utensils and work spaces be absolutely clean, but also the tops of metal cans and jars as well as the pressure canner should be free from any deposits of food bits that could prevent a complete seal.

5 **Use only good equipment and supplies.** Remember that anything less than perfect equipment runs the danger of producing spoiled and contaminated food.

6 **Don't be talked into new-fangled and untested methods.** The U.S. Department of Agriculture cautions that there is but one way to can meat -- by using the pressure canner -- and such other methods as oven or microwave canning, processing in the boiling water bath, use of a steamer without pressure, or the open kettle method are dangerous methods and should be avoided completely.

7 **Remember the two magic temperatures when canning meat: 170°F** - at this temperature negative enzyme action on food has been halted. It is also the minimum temperature when air will be expelled from containers and their contents. This is the temperature when spores of yeasts and molds are stopped dead in their tracks. **240°F** is the temperature that kills bacteria that can contaminate food. It is also the temperature that kills botulism spores. AND THIS TEMPERATURE CAN ONLY BE ARRIVED AT SAFELY UNDER PRESSURE, which is why you must have a pressure canner.

8 **Be alert for a perfect seal.** More about this later.

9 And finally, quoting from the U.S. Department of Agriculture Home and Garden Bulletin No. 162:

". . . If a canned food shows any sign of

spoilage — bulging can ends, leakage, spurting liquid, off-odor, or mold—**do not use it.** Do not even taste it."

And, we would add, don't feed it to your pets either; bury it fast!

10 **A fool-proof test to check meat, poultry, and fish that has been canned is to boil it for 15-20 minutes in an open kettle.** If a foul odor occurs, the food is spoiled and should not even be tasted. Use this test whenever you have any doubt about the safety of canned meats; in fact it is a good test for anyone to use after his first experience with canning meat anyway.

Cleaning Utensils and The Work Area

Everything that touches meat must be clean, and we mean absolutely clean, for bacteria will flourish otherwise with resulting food spoilage and contamination. Take the following precautions both before and after handling meat.

All metal objects such as knives, pans, saucepans, enamelware, and porcelain utensils that will be used must be washed thoroughly in hot, soapy water, then rinsed with boiling water.

Wooden surfaces and wood equipment such as working boards or butcher's blocks and wooden spoons must be scraped if necessary to remove all traces of dirt and foreign material. Then disinfect them with a chlorine disinfectant such as bleach diluted according to directions on the container. The chlorine disinfectant should remain on the surfaces for 15-30 minutes; then washed off and rinsed with boiling water. Treat food grinders accordingly.

Cloths you use should be washed with soapy water and rinsed with boiling water.

What Method of Canning To Choose?

Actually there are no methods to choose from when canning meat. There is only one, and it is mandatory -- the steam pressure method. No other is recommended at all. Even though some old books that were published before the pressure canner was invented mention other methods, these other methods should not be attempted. No responsible person would dare suggest that meat, poultry, and fish be canned by any method other than by steam pressure.

But just for general information, and in order to win an occasional argument, we are listing below the three methods by which food in general may be canned. They will help you see why the steam pressure method is the only one that is safe to use for meat products.

1 **Steam-pressure method.** For canning meat and low-acid foods including such vegetables as beets, corn, beans, and carrots. With this method, as we have already stated, the food in metal cans or glass jars must be processed at a temperature of 240°F, and the only way this temperature can be obtained safely is to use steam pressure of at least ten pounds (at sea level). And a special pressure canner designed for this purpose will do it.

2 **Water-bath method.** This method is for acid foods, such as tomatoes and fruits. With this method food is put into metal cans or jars, sealed, and then placed in a deep kettle or other utensil, filled with water to come a couple inches over the tops of the containers; then the water is left to boil for a prescribed length of time. The water can never become hotter than boiling (212° F), but this is hot enough to kill the organisms that would cause low-acid food to spoil.

3 **Open-kettle method.** This method is primarily for jams, jellies, preserves, relishes, and some pickles. Such food has a high enough content of sugar or vinegar to help preserve it. It is first cooked in an open kettle (hence the name of "open-kettle") for a prescribed length of time; then put into sterilized jars (not metal cans) and sealed.

How To Select Proper Metal Cans and Glass Jars

Meat, fish, and game may be successfully canned in either metal cans or in glass jars. Which you choose is up to you, and at the end of this discussion we list the advantages and disadvantages of each.

But bear in mind that in addition to having the basic container which holds the food, you must also have a cover and a way to seal the cover completely on to the container.

Metal Cans

Metal cans are usually made of reclaimed metal with a layer of tin on the outside as well as on the inside, hence the name "tin" cans.

There are three different kinds of tin cans:

C-enamel lined cans, primarily for low-acid foods containing sulfur and for fish
R-enamel lined cans, primarily for acid foods
Plain tin-lined cans, for just about everything

Plain tin cans are best for all meat, poultry, and fish.

Check to see that cans are in perfect condition without dents or holes, and that the lids with gaskets are in perfect condition to assure a perfect seal.

Remember that cans and lids may be used only once; then discarded for good.

While metal cans should be washed in plain hot water before being filled, their lids should not be washed for fear of disturbing their gaskets. However, lids should be wiped or rinsed carefully in hot water.

You will have to decide which of the various sizes of cans you wish to use; the size you select should bear some relationship to the number of people you plan to feed; otherwise you will have to store unused food in the refrigerator after cans are opened. The size of can may also require different processing times, for the more food in a can, the longer it takes to cook and to destroy all harmful organisms.

The most commonly used cans are the following:
No. 2, which holds 2½ cups
No. 2½, which holds 3½ cups
No. 3, which holds 4 cups.

Glass Jars

Described below are several types of glass jars used for canning. Remember that canning jars must withstand a high degree of heat (240°F under pressure); so don't allow yourself to be satisfied with just any old jar; be sure you have jars that are specifically made for home canning.

1 **Glass jars with glass lids.** These are not too common now, and glass lids are becoming harder and harder to find if you need them. The glass lid fits over a rubber jar ring, and a wire bail arrangement fits into a groove on the outside top of the glass lid; then a clamp arrangement allows the top to be drawn air-tight on to the ring.

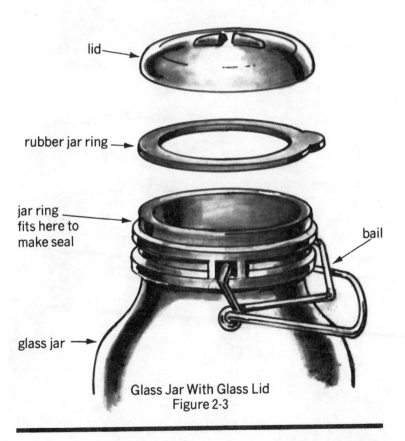

lid

rubber jar ring

jar ring fits here to make seal

bail

glass jar

Glass Jar With Glass Lid
Figure 2-3

2 **Glass jars with porcelain-lined tops (lids)** that are screwed on. This requires that the glass jar have a glass thread instead of the wire bail and clamp arrangement. The rubber ring is placed on the shoulder of the glass jar just below the threads. The top, which has metal threads on the sides, is screwed on to the glass threads of the jar. This type of jar and top is not too common now either. Jars with screw-on tops are often referred to as "Mason" jars.

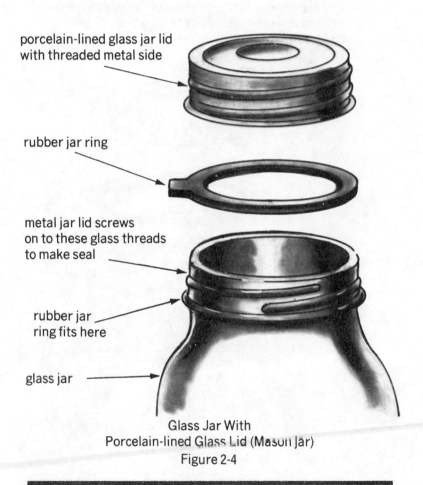

porcelain-lined glass jar lid
with threaded metal side

rubber jar ring

metal jar lid screws
on to these glass threads
to make seal

rubber jar
ring fits here

glass jar

Glass Jar With
Porcelain-lined Glass Lid (Mason Jar)
Figure 2-4

3 Next we have a **clear glass lid,** which, like the one opposite, is screwed down on to a rubber ring by means of a metal band being screwed on to the glass threads around the top of the jar. After the jar is processed and sealed, the metal band may be removed if you wish.

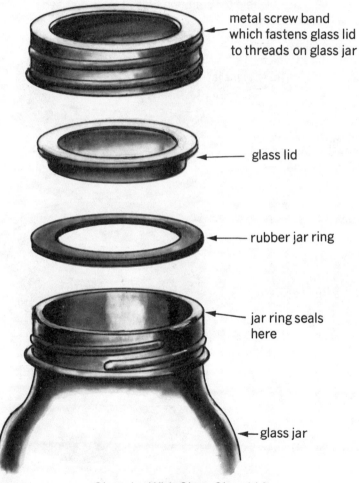

metal screw band which fastens glass lid to threads on glass jar

glass lid

rubber jar ring

jar ring seals here

glass jar

Glass Jar With Clear Glass Lid
Figure 2-5

4 Finally we have a **glass jar with glass threads** as
   above, but instead of a glass lid we have a metal lid,
   called a "dome" lid, with self-sealing compound on
   the underside. This rests directly on the open top of
   the jar and is held in place during processing by a
   metal band screwed on to the glass threads. With
   this type of jar the band may be removed completely
   after processing when the jar is sealed. This is
   currently the most common type of glass jar used
   for canning.

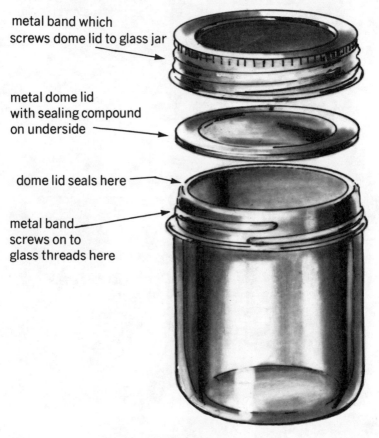

metal band which
screws dome lid to glass jar

metal dome lid
with sealing compound
on underside

dome lid seals here

metal band
screws on to
glass threads here

Glass Jar With Metal Dome Lid
Figure 2-6

Jars with the metal dome lids may have their tops screwed down completely before processing inasmuch as there still is plenty of escape available for air during processing, and as the air is expelled and the food shrinks somewhat, the vacuum created inside makes the seal. And after cooling, the metal band may be removed completely for storage and re-used.

With the other types of jars mentioned above (numbers 1 - 3) they must not be completely sealed before processing. Thus, the clamp on the glass jar with bail must not be tightened; the metal bands on the jars with glass lids and porcelain-lined lids must be tightened fully as soon as the jars are packed, then loosened one-quarter turn to allow air to escape during processing. Once processing is completed, they must be screwed down tight before the jars are cooled.

Here are a few hints about using glass jars:
1 Like metal cans, glass jars come in several sizes; so **be sure to select the sizes that are most convenient for the amount of food you are likely to use soon after opening.**
2 It is much easier to pack a jar that has a nice wide

opening at the top than one with a narrow opening. Likewise a wide opening makes it much easier to remove the contents after the jar is opened.

3 There are on the market now jars that are referred to as "can or freez" jars. In general they are much like the jar number 4 mentioned above except that the shape is tapered with the wider end at the top. These are much easier to fill and remove contents from than most other types of jars. Furthermore, they have been made to withstand freezing temperatures as well as hot temperatures; so they may be used interchangeably for canning or for freezing. The taper allows frozen food to be removed even before it is thawed. (More about this in the chapter on freezing.)

4 Be sure to **check that your glass jars are in good condition.** Unless they are free from nicks* and cracks on the lids, do not use them or you may have trouble with the seal. Check bands and rubbers, too, to be certain they are perfect.

5 Remember that rubber jar rings and metal lids must never be used a second time. Always use new ones.

6 Glass jars used for canning meat, poultry, and fish do not have to be sterilized before use. Why? Because they and their contents are processed at 240° F, which is greater than boiling (212° F), and jars along with their contents, are automatically sterilized during the processing. But jars and bands should be washed thoroughly with soapy water and rinsed; so should glass lids. And rubber rings and metal lids should be wiped clean before using.

7 The most common sizes of glass jars for canning hold either a pint or a quart although two-quart size jars are quite available; but processing time will have to be adjusted to compensate for the added volume when the large size jars are used.

---

*If nicks are minor, the jars and lids will still be okay for making home-made root beer! (Great on a hot day!)

GLASS JARS AND METAL CANS

Advantages and Disadvantages

Glass Jars
1 Jars, glass lids, and metal bands may be used over again.
2 No special equipment is required just for glass jars.
3 They do not stack, but store well side by side.
4 Initial cost is moderate and is not repeated since jars may be re-used.
5 Display contents of jars well.
6 Must be stored in a cool, dry, and dark place to prevent light from discoloring contents.
7 Must be cooled gradually lest they break due to change of temperature.
8 Jars with metal dome lids may be sealed completely before processing in the pressure canner; other jars should not be completely sealed beforehand.

Metal Cans
1 Neither cans nor lids may be re-used.
2 A can sealer is required.
3 They stack well and may be stored side by side.
4 Initial cost is moderate and is repeated since cans may not be re-used.
5 Do not display well since contents cannot be seen.
6 Must be stored in a cool and dry place. Needs not be dark since sun cannot shine on contents.
7 Should be cooled rapidly so not to cook the contents longer than recommended.
8 Cans should be completely sealed before processing in pressure canner.

How To Pack Cans and Jars

Meats to be Canned

As we noted previously, practically any kind of meat, including game, fish, and poultry may be canned successfully and easily providing simple and basic instructions are followed to the "T." The United States Department of Agriculture* mentions the following as being the most popular for canning:

- Beef, veal, mutton, lamb, pork
- Chicken, duck, goose, guinea, squab, turkey
- Rabbit
- Game birds
- Small-game animals
- Large-game animals

Large-game animals are treated the same as beef; small-game animals and rabbits are treated as poultry. Poultry and rabbits and small-game birds may even be canned with bone in.

The tender cuts such as steaks and roasts are excellent to can. So are stew meat and ground meat, which are generally from the less tender cuts and trimmings containing some connective tissue. Bony pieces are excellent for soups. Hearts and tongues may be canned; and while pork shoulders and hams may be, too, they are usually cured for smoking. Pork loins and meat from spareribs are excellent for canning.

Since fat is not desirable in canned meats, for it often prevents making a good seal, it should be trimmed away as much as possible, and cuts with considerable amounts of fat should be avoided.

The U.S. Department of Agriculture figures that for each one-quart jar you will need these quantities of untrimmed meat or meat with bone:

Beef:
Round . . . . 3 to 3½ pounds
Rump . . . . 5 to 5½ pounds
Pork Loin . . . . 5 to 5½ pounds
Chicken:
Canned with bone . . . . 3 to 4½ pounds
Canned without bone . . . . 5½ to 6¼ pounds

*Home and Garden Bulletin No. 106

Condition of Meat

Remember, too, that chilled meat is easier to handle than meat not chilled; and this is true when canning, too.

Since small pieces pack better than large, you may wish to cut small portions, but they will pack much easier and you will get more into a container if cut lengthwise of the grain. Large fleshy pieces should be rolled when possible.

But always pack loosely in order that air will be completely expelled and the meat completely cooked during processing.

Expelling Air

It is necessary for reasons we have mentioned earlier to remove air from containers and from the meat in order to obtain a perfect seal and to prevent spoilage from organisms in the air. This is referred to as "expelling" or "exhausting" the air.

We have said that meat, poultry, and fish must be processed under pressure at 240° F. Since the tops of glass jars are not completely sealed until processing is completed and the jars are cooled, the processing procedure actually exhausts or removes the air. However this can be speeded up and made more efficient sometimes if expelling, or exhausting, the air takes place before jars are actually put into the pressure canner. The procedure with metal cans is a bit different since they have to be completely sealed before they go into the pressure canner for processing; therefore under certain conditions, too, they are exhausted before being sealed.

To do this requires that containers of food be brought to a temperature of 170° F before being put into the pressure canner. Therefore after glass jars are filled to within an inch of the top (and no more) and metal cans are filled to the rim, they are placed in a large covered container without their tops on and allowed to boil until a thermometer placed in the middle of the cans or jars registers 170° F. Then after their rims have been carefully cleaned of any residue or bits of fat or meat, the tin cans must be sealed completely, and the lids put on the glass jars as we discussed on page 27; next into the pressure canner they go for processing.

Here is a good place to slow down a bit and ask ourselves a few questions:

1 Why did we have to bring the contents of the metal cans and glass jars to 170° F? Because 170° F is the minimum temperature when air can be expelled from the container and from the food in the container. Also at this temperature negative enzyme action has been halted, and the negative action of the spores of yeasts and molds stopped.

2 Why do we fill the metal cans to their rims and the glass jars to within one inch of their tops? Metal cans are filled to the top so there will be no room for air in the cans once they are sealed; this is necessary since they are sealed before going into the pressure canner. The glass jars are not sealed tight before being processed in the pressure canner (except jars with metal dome lids); if they were filled to the top, juices and small bits of their contents would bubble out during processing, messing up and endangering a good seal. Leaving space (not filling to the top) is referred to as leaving "headspace" or "headroom." For meats, poultry, and fish we should always leave an inch of headroom in glass jars.

3 What should you do if you do not have a thermometer? The best answer is to buy one! If that is impossible, continue boiling the filled cans or jars in the container until the contents are medium done. But it is best to invest in a rod-type thermometer or borrow one from a neighbor.

4 What else does expelling, or exhausting, do? It helps prevent changes in the flavor of food after being canned.

5 Is it always necessary to heat cans and glass jars filled with meat to 170° F before putting them in the pressure canner for processing? No; if meat and meat products are hot and already cooked, it is not necessary to go through this step. This step is used in those instances where the containers are packed with raw food.

Packing

This may be done in one of two ways: the raw pack method (not usually recommended) or the hot pack method.

1 **Raw Pack Method.** This means that meat is packed in cans or glass jars, with no added liquid, before it is cooked; thus it is uncooked or raw. Cans and jars must then be heated to 170°F as discussed above before being processed in the pressure canner.

2 **Hot Pack Method.** This involves pre-cooking meat before packing it in cans or jars. Again, contents must be at least 170°F before the metal cans are sealed and before the lids are placed on the glass jars. And pre-cooked meat must be kept hot at all times.

Here are some hints on packing food into cans and jars:

1 It is best to pack rather loosely; otherwise a certain amount of the liquid may be lost. This is especially true in the case of glass jars.

2 If hot pack instructions call for adding liquid, be sure it is boiling hot. Packing raw foods usually calls for adding water.

3 If you wish to add a broth as liquid, put some meat in a pan, cover it with cold water, and let it simmer until the meat becomes tender; then strain off the broth, cool it, and remove the fat. It is then ready to be reheated and added to the pre-cooked meat.

4 If you use glass jars that have straight sides, or sides tapered outward toward the top, they will be much easier to pack.

5 You may use salt for flavor, but other flavors, such as herbs and spices, will likely lose value or become bitter. Salt should be used in about the following amounts:

> ½ teaspoon for #2 cans (two and one-half cups)
> ¾ teaspoon for #2½ cans
> > (three and one-half cups)
> 1 teaspoon for #3 cans (one quart)

Sealing Containers

Once the cans and jars are packed, they should be put in a covered container and brought to 170° F as described above if you are using the raw pack method; then transferred to the pressure canner for processing. If you are using the hot pack method, the containers should be capped, again as we have described above, and put in the pressure canner for processing.

How To Process Cans And Jars

When we discussed necessary equipment (pages 14-17), we went into considerable detail about the pressure canner. But perhaps you will want to review it now before starting to process your canned products. And certainly you will want to read the manufacturer's instructions that came with your canner. There are a number of different makes of pressure canners, and the instructions for one do not necessarily apply to all others.

After metal cans and glass jars are filled and are ready for the canner, they should be placed on the rack at the bottom, but it is important to arrange them so they do not touch its sides or the sides of one another. If steam is prevented from circulating evenly and completely around each can or jar, cold spots may develop, causing food spoilage due to incomplete processing.

Put two or three inches of water in the canner (or as otherwise suggested by the manufacturer), tighten the cover on securely, place over heat, and allow steam to come out of the canner through the petcock or other prescribed opening for a full ten minutes. Why for ten minutes? Because all air must be driven from the canner by the steam; again, if air is not driven out, cold spots may develop to cause food spoilage.

Once the heat has risen to 240°F on the thermometer gauge (or to ten pounds pressure if you have a pressure gauge instead of a thermometer), you must begin timing the processing.

Instructions with the canner, with your jars, or in your canning book will indicate how long the temperature must be held at 240°F or at ten pounds pressure. Be certain that heat does not fluctuate during processing, for fluctuations can cause liquid to escape from glass jars and prevent a seal, and all your work will have been done for nothing.

As soon as time is up, remove the canner from the heat at once to prevent any further cooking of the contents of the cans and jars; else the contents may become mushy. If you are using glass jars, allow the pressure to return to zero, carefully remove the petcock or other device for releasing steam after pressure has returned to zero, open the canner as you hold the cover facing you to shield you from steam coming at you, and remove the glass jars, preferably with tongs designed for that purpose.

Do not try to cool the canner to zero with cold water! This, too, causes jars to lose their liquid and break the seal.

If you are using metal cans, as soon as processing time is up and the heat is turned off, open the petcock to release all the steam; then open the canner and remove the cans. To allow cans to remain in the canner longer would result in unnecessary further cooking of their contents.

How To Cool, Label, and Store

Cooling

As soon as jars are out of the canner, complete the seal if necessary. Remember that cooling increases the seal. Jars should be placed on a rack or soft surface to cool and kept away from drafts. Some say not to cover them with a soft thin blanket or towels; I disagree. I have seen hot jars crack when a door was suddenly opened letting in a draft. As soon as jars are cool, remove the metal bands if they come off easily, and clean and store them for next use.

In the case of metal cans, which have been sealed prior to processing, dunk them in cold water as soon as they are removed from the canner and continue changing the water until the cans are cool. Cans require fast cooling to prevent further cooking of their contents. Cans should be stored in a staggered fashion for final cooling and drying.

It is important to examine the seals of both cans and jars about twenty-four hours after removing from the canner. Tops of cans and metal lids of jars will be slightly indented inward if the seal is good. You should also tap the metal lids with a smooth metal object such as a spoon and listen for a clear metalic ring. Check the seams of the cans, turning them to inspect for leaks, as you should have done with the jars.

If you find a leaky can or jar, either eat the contents right away or heat the contents, repack, and reprocess again for the full time. DO NOT REPROCESS FISH PRODUCTS.

Labeling

You should label your containers with date (and with contents if you use metal cans). If any can bulges a bit from overpacking, note it on the label to prevent confusion later with one that may have spoiled. And if you have had to reprocess a container of meat, you might do well to indicate that also on the label and identify it as one to use early.

Storing

Cans and jars should be stored in a cool, dry place. It is important, too, that jars not be exposed to light, for color changes in the food may occur as a result. We said cool, but don't let the containers freeze; else seals may be broken. We said dry, for dampness can erode metal lids and cans.

Food Spoilage

If there is any fear that canned food has spoiled, boil it in an open pan for 15-20 minutes and note the odor. Boiling usually intensifies the odor of spoiled foods. If there is any doubt, destroy it without even tasting or allowing your pets to taste.

Summary

It is probably a good idea to note some topics we have just been discussing which are of prime importance in canning meat, poultry, and fish to assure success. Each one is quite simple in itself, but very important if we want canned food that is free from contamination, well sealed, good to look at, tasteful, and nutritious.

- Maximum cleanliness at all times
- Only good quality meat
- Keep meat cool until ready to can
- Proper containers in good condition
- New jar rubbers and metal lids always
- Always can under steam pressure of at least ten pounds (240°F)
- Know your pressure canner
- Proper headspace, or headroom
- Proper sealing
- Proper expelling of air
- Proper timing of temperature or pressure while processing
- Tops of jars and rims of cans always free from foreign matter
- No short-cuts of proper procedures
- Cool, dark, and dry storage
- Always check seals before storage

Now you may stand back and congratulate yourself for having done a good job of canning. It wasn't so hard after all, was it?

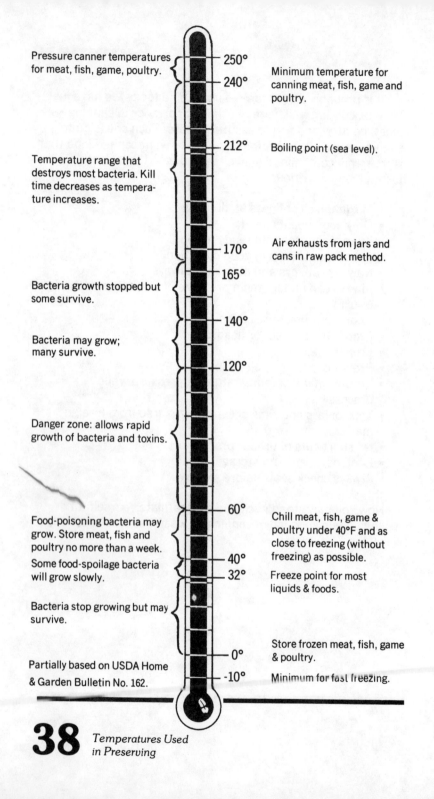

Pressure canner temperatures for meat, fish, game, poultry.

250°

240° — Minimum temperature for canning meat, fish, game and poultry.

212° — Boiling point (sea level).

Temperature range that destroys most bacteria. Kill time decreases as temperature increases.

170° — Air exhausts from jars and cans in raw pack method.

165°

Bacteria growth stopped but some survive.

140°

Bacteria may grow; many survive.

120°

Danger zone: allows rapid growth of bacteria and toxins.

60° — Chill meat, fish, game & poultry under 40°F and as close to freezing (without freezing) as possible.

Food-poisoning bacteria may grow. Store meat, fish and poultry no more than a week.

40°

Some food-spoilage bacteria will grow slowly.

32° — Freeze point for most liquids & foods.

Bacteria stop growing but may survive.

0° — Store frozen meat, fish, game & poultry.

-10° — Minimum for fast freezing.

Partially based on USDA Home & Garden Bulletin No. 162.

38 *Temperatures Used in Preserving*

3
FREEZING

Freezing is a method of preserving or storing food in a frozen state during which time the growth activity of bacteria, molds, yeasts, and enzymes is slowed down or stopped. During freezing, water in the meat is transformed into ice crystals.

Contrary to general opinion, freezing does not kill most bacteria; bacteria will commence to grow again after meat is thawed. (The bacteria causing trichinosis is killed during freezing, but only at certain temperatures and over a period of time; this will be discussed in the chapter on pork.)

And, contrary to general opinion, freezing does not improve the quality of meat; it may temporarily (up to four to eight weeks) improve its tenderness, however.

There are certain requirements that must be met if meat is to be frozen properly; any attempts to avoid these requirements only court failure.

Meat must be wrapped in air-tight containers, i.e. moisture-, odor-, and vapor-proof. Why?

1. Because moisture (ice crystals) in meat must not be allowed to dry out since it must be returned to the meat as juice when the meat is thawed. Such drying out is known as "freezer burn."
2. Because vapors from outside sources must not be allowed to enter the meat and add to moisture already in it.
3. Because natural odors of meat must not be allowed

Note: Unless specified otherwise, the word "meat" in this chapter refers to all meat: fish, game, and poultry being included.

to enter other products in the freezer; neither should odors from other products be allowed to enter the meat.

Just about anything that may be canned may also be frozen: cooked or raw, bone in or bone out, smoked or unsmoked. And probably the quality of no food is better preserved by freezing than is that of seafood.

It has been proven that by far the best way to maintain the good color, flavor, and quality of meat is to fast-freeze it (some call this "flash" freezing or "blast" freezing). Fast-freezing it makes for smaller ice crystals throughout the meat, preserving its uniformity.

Some say meat should be fast-frozen at 0°F or lower; but the United States Department of Agriculture most often recommends -10°F or lower. Most commercial slaughterhouses fast-freeze at 20°F below zero and sometimes even at 40°F below. Following fast-freezing, meat should be stored at 0°F or, even better, at -10°F.

Chest-type freezers, when set to their lowest point, can usually cool to well under -15°F. Upright freezers frequently cannot go quite so low. The best way to determine if your freezer is capable of fast-freezing is to place a thermometer in the compartment or area where the manufacturer recommends that food be fast-frozen preparatory to storing and take a reading. If you find that your freezer cannot achieve the degree of cold you want for fast-freezing, try to find a freezer locker plant in your area and have the fast-freezing done there; then you can store the frozen food in your own freezer.

You might do well to consider having your meat fast-frozen at the locker plant anyway if you have large quantities to be done, for even when set to their lowest point, home freezers frequently have trouble fast-freezing big quantities of meat as rapidly as it should be done.

There is of course a limit to the length of time that frozen meat maintains its good quality. To draw on government* experience again, the following table shows the maximum

---

*USDA Home and Garden Bulletin Nos. 70 and 93 and Canada, Department of Agriculture Publication 892.

recommended lengths of time meat should be stored frozen at 0°F before it should be consumed.

Beef	Up to 12 months (depending on cuts)
Veal	Up to 8 months (depending on cuts)
Lamb	Up to 12 months (depending on cuts)
Pork	Up to 8 months (depending on cuts)
Fish	6 to 9 months
Ground meat	3 months
Sausage	3 to 4 months
Uncooked poultry:	
Whole chicken or turkey	12 months
Whole duck and goose	6 months
Poultry, cut up	3 months
Giblets	3 months
Cured meat (ham, bacon, corned beef)	1 to 2 months

In the above table you will note that sausage does not keep long comparatively; sausage and uncooked cured meats do not freeze too satisfactorily; primarily because salt, which is in sausage and which is part of the curing process, has a tendency to speed the rate at which meat becomes rancid when frozen.

Why Freeze Meat?

There are certain advantages and disadvantages with whatever process of storing food one uses; each person must decide individually which method is best for his own purposes.

The advantages of freezing over canning are about as follows:

- Many believe the nutrients in meat are retained longer if meat is frozen than if it is processed in other ways.

- Freezing is generally faster.
- Freezing is less expensive in terms of equipment and material needed (if we do not include investment in a freezer).
- Freezing is simpler to do than canning.
- Frozen food generally has a greater quality of freshness.

But these advantages have to be weighed against the following:
- The cost of a freezer, or the cost of renting a food locker if indeed one is even available.
- It takes more time to thaw frozen food properly than it does to open a can or jar of food. In a rush this might be important.
- Once food is canned, there is little or no further upkeep in cost. Freezing involves the continued cost of electricity to maintain food in a frozen state, or rental charges if in a community locker.
- It is simpler to leave home for a month's vacation if food is stored in cans than when frozen for fear that electric power may fail and contents of the freezer may require emergency treatment to survive. (This fear is less likely, however, if food is stored in a community locker.)
- Some foods will not maintain their quality so long when frozen as when canned.
- Canned foods can be stored longer than frozen foods.
- Canned foods are easier to transport over distance. If you plan to move, can, don't freeze.

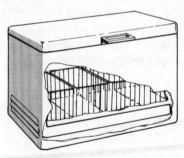

What Meat to Freeze?

Somehow frozen food seems to have a freshness about it that one often misses in canned food. And, as we have indicated above, anything that may be canned may also be frozen so long as it is of high quality.

Nevertheless some things do not keep so long when frozen as when canned. Cooked meats and poultry and mixtures with sauces and gravies encourage the growth of bacteria. Stew meat and ground meat should be consumed within two to three months after freezing. Cutlets and chops are best if not stored frozen longer than four months; the same is true for organ meats. Frozen cured meat takes no time at all to lose its quality, bacon lasting not over a month and ham usually not over two. Frozen cooked hams will keep their quality considerably longer than frozen uncooked hams.

As with canning, there are economies to be had in freezing food whenever it is most available, or available at the best prices. Research has also shown that the best economies in the use of frozen food are achieved also when food is constantly being added to the freezer or locker and when food is constantly being consumed.

Necessary Equipment

We'll assume you have a home freezer, or access to a community food locker, for fast-freezing and storage of your meats.

At the start of this chapter we said it is necessary that food to be frozen be contained in such a way to make it moisture-, odor-, and vapor-proof. Therefore it will not pay to economize by using just any old material around the house to wrap your meat in; that will not be economy at all when frozen food spoils or loses its quality. Use only material that will seal your meat air-tight and prevent its drying out; therefore buy material that is made especially for home-freezing.

"Can or freez" jars are ideal for freezing meat since they may be made air-tight by screwing the band to the lids. Jars not made to be frozen should not be used, for they are likely to split as the contents expand when they are frozen; this is especially true of jars that taper inward at the top. Freezer jars as well as glazed pottery, plastic boxes, aluminum containers, and even tin or tin-enameled containers are great for packing meat into, especially cooked meat, because they may either be sealed air-tight by their tops, or the tops may be sealed on with special freezer tape. So, be sure to have plenty of freezer tape on hand.

There are a number of moisture-vapor-resistant "papers" made especially for the freezer, which you will want to have available: aluminum freezer foil (special heavy weight), cellophane-coated freezer paper, laminated-coated freezer paper, polyethylene-coated freezer paper, and polyethylene plastic. Read the instructions that come with them pertaining to wrapping and sealing.

Wax paper? Not for wrapping, but a good idea to put between chops and cuts that need to be separated during defrosting.

Moisture-vapor-resistant bags are available, too, and are very handy for wrapping fowl and small pieces of meat but not good for liquids. They are frequently of plastic or of coated or laminated freezer paper.

Some stockinette tubing is desirable to put over wrapped meat packages to prevent any tearing of the wrappings.

Finally, some rubber bands will come in handy, a marking pencil, and a sealing iron if instructions with the paper or bags recommend sealing with a hot iron. Yes, and maybe a wide-mouth funnel to use in filling containers.

Since you will wish to freeze meat in family-size units, containers should be selected on the basis of family size. Glass jars and freezer boxes are readily available in one-half pint, one pint, one and one-half pints and quart sizes.

Cleaning Utensils and Work Area
It is just as important to use as good sanitary methods when freezing foods as it is when canning; and the precautions of cleaning utensils, scrubbing the work areas, and maintaining a

high level of cleanliness are the same as for canning. Since we have already discussed this on pp. 19-20, there is no point in repeating it here, but it would be well to review those pages. Remember that whenever food is handled, the spread of bacteria is increased. Remember, too, that unlike in the process of canning, bacteria are not killed when food is frozen; they are merely put into an inactive stage ready to continue their bad work as soon as food starts to thaw. For this reason it is perhaps even more important to be certain that all sanitary precautions are followed and maintained when freezing food.

How to Prepare Meat Before Wrapping

Since we know that meat handles better after it is chilled, and since we also know that chilling adds to its tenderness at least temporarily, meat must be chilled before being wrapped for freezing.

Before they are cut up, carcasses should be hung and chilled to below 40°F within twenty-four hours after slaughter, but a temperature just above freezing seems best (33°F to 34°F). Carcasses should touch nothing when hung, nor should they touch each other; else air will not circulate around them completely, thus heightening the possibility of negative action from harmful bacteria.

Following is the recommended chilling time for various kinds of meats:

Beef	5 to 7 days (or even longer)
Pork	1 to 2 days
Veal	1 to 2 days
Lamb	5 to 7 days
Poultry	12 hours minimum
Fish	Chill immediately when caught and process as soon as possible.

Following chilling, carcasses should be cut into the portions you want for the freezer. It is best to think of portion sizes in terms of the number of people who will be eating it and cut the portions accordingly, for family size packages are also the right sizes for maximum economy.

Information on cutting up carcasses will be found in the later chapters that pertain to specific kinds of meat.

How to Wrap and Seal Meat for Freezing

The low humidity of freezers tends to dry the meat out; this tendency is a main reason for sealing it in proper wrappings or containers to retard this effect. But wrapped meat should be wrapped tightly, also, to squeeze out all air possible; for normal air contains bacteria and other enemies of food. If meat is packed in rigid containers, it should be packed tight for the same reason.

And in order that moisture does not escape through the wrappings, or that vapor and odors do not penetrate it, the proper paper must be moisture-vapor-resistant paper. If meat is packed in rigid containers, they, too, should be moisture-vapor-resistant.

A couple layers of wax paper between individual chops, fillets, steaks, and the like will make it much easier to separate them later when defrosting.

So, again, wrap everything tight, pushing out all the air possible, and making the wrappings conform to the shape of the cuts being wrapped.

Moisture-vapor-resistant paper works best when a drugstore fold is used as illustrated in Figure 3-1.

Another very effective wrap is the one called the butcher's wrap, and this is illustrated at Figure 3-2.

Packages should be sealed with regular freezer tape to cover the seams completely. Unless rigid containers have screw tops or other means of sealing them air-tight, their tops, too, should be sealed with freezer tape. Jars made especially for freezing (such as "can or freez" jars) are extremely useful and their shape is tapered outward toward the top to facilitate emptying their contents during thawing. Other rigid containers such as plastic boxes, glazed pottery, and tin-enameled ones

Paper is pulled tight around meat. The seam is sealed with the fold.

Ends of the wrap are folded back under the package and the main fold is sealed with freezer tape. The ends are also taped back when folded.

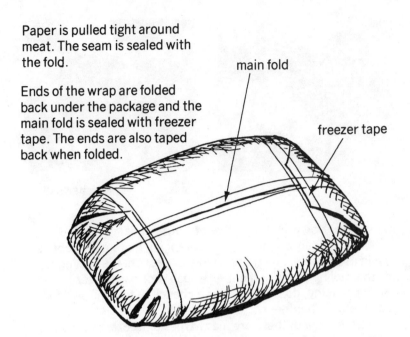

main fold

freezer tape

Drugstore Fold
Figure 3-1

may be used and work well, especially for ground meat, and meat with sauces and gravies. Leave at least a half inch of headroom for expansion during freezing in rigid containers packed with liquids and sauces. These containers are also good for small cuts such as chicken livers and thighs.

Special freezer bags are very useful, too, for a collection of small cuts (again, chicken thighs); and occasionally a cut of meat that is difficult to wrap goes well inside a freezer bag; the bag is then heat-sealed, or twisted and tied with string or a rubber band.

If instructions with your freezer paper or containers require heat-sealing, you will need a hot iron or special tool to do this; follow instructions that come with your supplies.

There is frequently danger that wrappers of frozen meat may be torn when packages are moved or rearranged in the freezer, thus allowing air to penetrate the otherwise air-tight package. Covering such packages with stockinette tubing

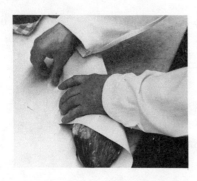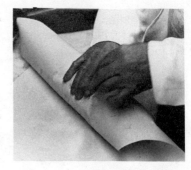

Butcher's Wrap

before freezing will protect them from such damage.

Be absolutely certain that all packaging material is kept as clean as possible, and that no moisture covers the sealing tape or the sealing edges of the freezer paper or bags; freezing, unlike canning, does not give us a chance to test the seal for complete air-tightness.

As mentioned, there are many types of freezer papers, containers, and sealing tapes; and new ones are constantly being perfected and marketed. We should expect others to be available perhaps even while this book is being printed. Therefore the instructions that come with your supplies should always be read carefully and followed carefully.

Labeling

When all your individual packages are in the freezer, unless you have some way to identify them, you will have trouble locating the ones you want to serve at some future date.

One way to overcome this would-be problem is to number each package with a marking pencil or pen (do not use ink that penetrates the wrapping paper; some inks are very strong); then describe in a notebook what each numbered package contains.

Another way is to make a notation right on the package itself.

Here is what you will want to know:

Figure 3-2

Kind of meat (such as beef, pork, lamb, venison, trout)

Name of cut (chops, liver, roast, fillets)

Date frozen (very important since this will assist you in using older cuts first)

Special information (such as "with gravy," "cooked," "for three people," "from Sally Perry's prize beef ")

It is a great convenience to have a freezer inventory outside the freezer, noting when containers are added and removed. Or keep this information in your notebook, mentioned above.

It is also desirable to indicate if the meat has been refrozen, for refrozen meat should always be used first.

How to Freeze and Store

All food must have a fast or "flash" freeze before packages are stacked in the freezer for storage. This means freezing the packages solid at a temperature of -10°F or lower.

Several hours before you are ready to fast-freeze, lower the temperature control so the freezer chest will be at -10°F when your packages are ready to be frozen.

Try to schedule freezing so not more than two pounds of food per each cubic foot of freezer space is fast-frozen at one time. And the packages should be placed on shelves or surfaces in the freezer chest nearest the freezing coils or cooling surfaces. Do not allow packages being frozen to touch each other, and certainly not to touch packages already frozen!

Spread them out well; and if speed is important, a fan in the chest to circulate the cold air will hasten matters.

Once all packages are fast-frozen, they should be stacked compactly with like contents grouped together for convenience.

Temperature controls may now be set back to 0°F, and packages may remain at that temperature until removed to be consumed.

Power Failure!

Occasionally the freezer may lose power either through a breakdown of the freezer itself or through general power failure.

If it can be determined that loss of power is only temporary, there is nothing to worry about. But if power is off for a day or more, or if there is no indication when power will be restored, you should be prepared to take some action.

Remedy #1 is not to open the freezer at all but to wait for power to be restored. But if loss of power is more than one day,

Remedy #2 should be considered. This requires placing about twenty-five pounds of dry ice on a sheet of cardboard over the top of the frozen packages in the freezer; then close the freezer tight. If it is about half full of food, this should hold the food frozen for two or three days. Even so, you should check every twenty-four hours to determine if more dry ice is required. If the freezer is practically full, food should remain frozen for three or four days.

Where to get dry ice? Look in the yellow pages of your phone book under ice cream manufacturers, refrigeration supply outlets, or look for companies that sell compressed gas and contact them. Your own electric utility company may be able to advise you where dry ice may be obtained.

Remedy #3 would be to remove the frozen packages and place them in a public food locker if available. But remember to wrap the food with newspapers and blankets heavily so it will not thaw out en route to the locker.

Refreezing Meat

It is safe to refreeze meat that has started to thaw providing ice crystals remain in it. But under no circumstances should meat be refrozen if off-color or off-odor are noticed; destroy it at once without tasting by man or beast! In general refreezing reduces the quality of meat somewhat; so it should be noted on the label and used first. Meat that has been completely thawed should not be refrozen if it can be avoided.

Thawing Meat

It is best to thaw meat in the refrigerator in its original wrappings; this prevents evaporation of its natural juices. However it may be cooked whether or not it has thawed, but unthawed meat naturally requires more time to cook than does meat that has thawed. Other than that, it should be treated like fresh meat when being cooked. But cook it quickly following removal from the refrigerator; else dormant bacteria will get into action and start spoilage.

It seems rather meaningless to try to present a table here indicating how much time is required to thaw meat. So much depends on the temperature at which it was held in the freezer, the thickness of the meat, how it was wrapped, the temperature in your refrigerator, and a number of other factors. So do a little experimenting on your own and keep track of the thawing time of a few pieces, and you will be able to estimate quite closely the amount of time needed.

Of course, the defrost feature on microwave ovens have greatly simplified and quickened this process.

Summary of Hints and Precautions

- Freeze fresh and high quality meats only.
- Be sure meat is properly chilled before wrapping.
- Prepare and freeze meats promptly.
- Removing bones and excess fat will save freezer space. Removing fat also removes a cause for meat to become rancid.
- Fast-freeze all meat at least at -10°F, and lower is better.
- Store frozen meat at 0°F or lower.

- The lower the temperature the better the quality is maintained.
- Uneven temperatures cause frozen foods to lose quality.
- Never freeze stuffed poultry; remove stuffing and freeze it separately.
- Always thaw poultry in its wrapper to keep in its natural juices. Other meat is also best when thawed in its wrapper in the refrigerator.
- Uncooked cured meats lose their quality very fast when frozen.
- Meat must be sealed air-tight; this requires air-tight containers or wrappings in moisture-vapor-resistant papers.
- The drugstore fold is the tightest wrap to use, but the butcher's wrap is a very good way to wrap also.
- Headroom of ½" to ¾" is necessary when glass jars and rigid containers are used for liquids, meats in sauces, etc. and only slight headroom is needed for non-rigid containers with no liquid to allow for expansion during fast-freezing.
- A chest-type freezer is more efficient in terms of operation than an up-right freezer although not always so convenient to use.
- The best economy is achieved when the freezer is used to capacity.
- Know what remedies are possible to keep food frozen in the event that electric power is lost.
- Treat your freezer with great respect. Unless it is defrosted and maintained in accordance with the manufacturer's instructions, frozen food will not store well, its quality will deteriorate, and the cost of operation of the freezer will be excessive.

4
CURING

WHAT IS CURING?

Curing is the process of preserving meat for future needs primarily with the use of salt; a by-product of the curing process is the added flavor that curing imparts, especially when spices and herbs are used in the curing process. Curing is also a prelude to smoking meat; meat to be smoked in most instances should be cured before being smoked.

But curing is not just as simple as putting salt on meat, although it is still a very simple process and permits much room for personal experimentation and satisfaction.

To understand the process, we first need to be aware of some basic facts. **Almost all meats have a high percentage of water which must be removed to prevent spoilage, and the application of salt to meat extracts most of this water.** At the same time salt, as it invades the meat, produces an antibacterial action to preserve meat from spoiling. But meat cannot be preserved by curing at the snap of the finger; it takes time for salt to penetrate the meat thoroughly. The larger the pieces of meat, the longer the time required.

While ordinary course household salt or kosher salt is used (do not use common table salt), the action of salt alone tends to dry out meat, leaving it hard and very salty to the taste. And there may also be loss of color. So to counteract all this, sugar, or some other sweetener such as maple syrup or honey, is added to the salt to soften its overpowering effect and to induce good flavor. Saltpeter is also added not only as a meat preservative but also to fix the red color. And certain spices are frequently added to the salt mixture to enhance the flavor of the cured meat.

When all the various curing ingredients are mixed thoroughly and used on the meat in a dry state, it is called a **dry cure**. But we may mix them with pure water, in which case it is called a **brine** or a **sweet pickle cure** or a "wet" cure. Either way is efficient and gives fairly similar end results; however some people prefer working it dry while others prefer the brine method. The dry cure is usually a bit faster while the brine cure is usually more mild and less salty.

Saltpeter: Yes or No?

Saltpeter is an ingredient the United States Department of Agriculture lists for curing meats, and it is found in just about every recipe the USDA includes in its bulletins on cured meats. Saltpeter is supposed to do two things, as we mentioned above: fix the color of the meat to keep it red and retard the growth of potentially harmful bacteria. Chemically, saltpeter is either potassium nitrate or sodium nitrate (which is called "Chile saltpeter"). Since nitrates change to nitrites in our bodies, there is fear among many that it can be harmful to one's health and body systems, for nitrites have been charged with combining with the blood's hemoglobin to reduce its ability to carry oxygen throughout the body. Also, nitrites and protein (i.e. meatfoods) may form nitrosamines upon heating or during digestion. Nitrosamines are carcinogens, so it is best to limit consumption of cured meat.

Sometimes nitrates and nitrites are combined and used in combination for curing meats. The USDA continues to study the effects of these chemicals, and we might well see rulings made to limit their use in food.

Since the USDA includes the addition of saltpeter in its recipes, we have included it where curing meat is involved. But we would point out that there are those who believe that saltpeter may be harmful to the body to such an extent that it should, of course, be omitted entirely.

54 Curing

Those who advocate this maintain that the salt used in curing can very well limit the growth of harmful bacteria without having to depend on saltpeter, and that there is little other use for saltpeter except to fix color.

Curing: Getting Ready

Now to understand the process even better, let's go back and assume we have a freshly killed animal, and we'll follow forward the various steps in curing meat.

First the animal has to be bled completely, for blood spoils meat faster than anything else; and we will be working with this meat for quite some time before it is completely cured and possibly even later smoked.

Immediately after the animal is killed and drawn, the carcass must be chilled for several days (the length of time depending on the type and size of the animal; later chapters indicate how long animals should be chilled). Chilling not only makes the carcass easier to cut up, it also assures that bacterial and enzyme action is slowed up to allow time for the dry cure or the brine cure to penetrate the meat thoroughly and itself stop negative bacterial and enzyme action. So it is paramount that the chilling be thorough - clear through to and including the bones in the very middle of the carcass - in order that this negative action will be slowed down as much as possible. Chilling should be done as close to 32°F as possible without freezing, and most slaughterhouses feel that 34°F is ideal; but this is difficult to regulate on the farm; so **stay as close to 32°F as possible without freezing but well under 40°F.** If you do not have a near-by slaughterhouse to kill and chill your animal carcass, better wait until winter months to slaughter when cold weather will give you the kind of temperature you need for butchering at home.

One other reminder: **everything must be thoroughly clean and sanitary and maintained so throughout the curing process.** Better review what we have already said about this in the chapter on canning; the same precautions should be taken when curing.

What You Need To Do The Job

It is an easy thing to make a long list of equipment that is needed for practically anything that has to be done. This is the wrong way to go about it.

If a person is canning, freezing, or curing meat for the first time, he does not want to go into a big investment in utensils, for he may decide that processing meat is not the thing for him. But if, as we suspect, he finds processing a simple and interesting thing and a way to save money for the household, he will know once he has tried it what other pieces of equipment he would like to work with.

So when we list equipment, we list only the basic things. If others are needed, they are usually found around the house rather quickly or else borrowed from a neighbor.

For curing meat, here is what we think you ought to have:

- **A crock or hard-wood barrel** to do the curing in if you use the sweet pickle (wet) method, probably holding five or ten gallons minimum.
- **A box with holes in the bottom** (see Figure 4-1) to cure the meat in if you are using the dry cure.
- **A brine pump** if you wish to pump your meat (to be described later).
- **Other supplies** you may need you can easily find as you need them around the house.

Now let's assume you have cut up the chilled carcass and have selected the pieces you wish to have cured, perhaps some hams or some bacon or maybe some beef brisket for corning. We must now make a dry cure mixture or a sweet pickle, depending on which method you choose. Let's assume you wish a dry cure.

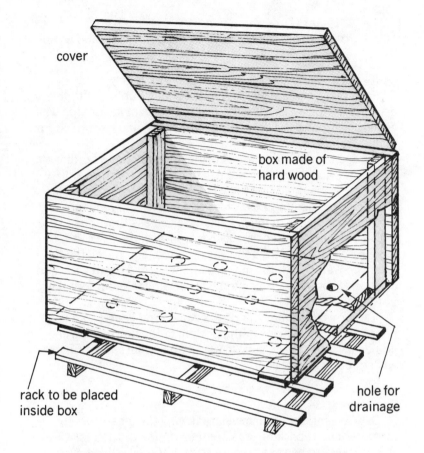

cover

box made of
hard wood

rack to be placed
inside box

hole for
drainage

Box for dry curing. Wooden rack rises meat off
bottom of box.

Figure 4-1

Dry Curing

In later chapters we shall indicate proportions of ingredients depending on the type of meat being used, but for the time being it is sufficient to say that a standard recipe for dry curing would include:

- **Salt**
- **Sugar**

- **Saltpeter** (?)
- Possibly some spices such as pepper, garlic, and some onion flavor.

All the ingredients should be mixed thoroughly.

Each piece of meat should be thoroughly rubbed with this dry mixture. Don't be afraid to use too much of it, rub it in well, especially around the bones and joint areas, and cover every bit of the outside of the meat with it.

Spread a good layer of the curing mixture on the bottom of a large box or container (do not use metal ones, for they will corrode). Place the largest pieces of meat at the bottom, skin side down, completely covering them with the dry mixture and not allowing pieces to touch each other unless they touch pieces that are also thoroughly covered with the dry salt mixture. Smaller pieces go toward the top, and finally the top layer is covered with the mixture and weighted down with a lid or cover. Here the curing meat will remain for about four days until it is "overhauled."

Earlier we said that salt draws water from meat; so it is important to have holes in the bottom of the box to allow the liquids to drain off. Be sure to set the box where the drainage will not damage any floor.

Overhauling

Overhauling simply involves removing the meat from the container and repacking it as before with the dry salt mixture and checking to be sure no bare spots show up, which, if they do, should be well rubbed with the dry salt mixture. Meat should remain in the second cure for two days per pound of meat; small pieces not quite so long. But remember that if the weather is very cold, curing time should be lengthened; and if very warm, shortened. No cut and dried rules can be imposed for curing time; so much depends on personal preference, thickness of meat, the weather, and other variable factors. And large pieces may need to be overhauled again, but for small pieces once is usually enough, after which they can be removed from the curing box. Personal experimentation and variables you are able to control will indicate the proper time needed for the cure to suit your taste.

Brine Cure

Perhaps you prefer to use the sweet pickle, or brine, cure instead of the dry cure. In that case the salt mixture you had previously mixed dry should be dissolved in cold water. Be sure it is pure water even if you have to boil it, for many bacteria found in normal drinking water will multiply and cause harm when they are in a sweet pickle cure. Also chlorinated water can spoil the taste of otherwise excellently cured meat. A good safety precaution is always to boil the water; then let it cool before it is used.

Most recipes for a sweet pickle will tell you how many cups or pounds of salt to put in the solution. Seldom do recipes call for a certain percentage of salt. For this reason we do not believe you will need a salinometer to measure the amount of

Hardwood barrel packed for brine cure. A well-seasoned barrel is also excellent for salting down pork fat and fish.

Figure 4-2

salt. Suffice it to know, however, that eight pounds of salt in four or four and a half gallons of water will give you about a 20% solution, which the USDA recommends for sweet pickling a ham. This solution is strong enough to stop the growth of most bacteria - even bacteria that can survive in some small amounts of salt - providing all other necessary precautions are taken.

A common way to measure the amount of salt, and one our grandparents used for many years, and which you will find in some old recipe books, was to add enough salt to the solution so an egg or a potato would float.

The more curing you do the more you will discover a certain solution that appeals to your taste; so you should not be satisfied just with the recipes others use; neither should you be so bold with one of your own that you throw caution to the winds and incur spoilage and disaster.

When well mixed and dissolved, the liquid brine should be put in a container to about one-third full, and the meat to be cured placed in it. Be certain the solution surrounds every piece of meat and that it covers well over the top pieces. Place a plate on the top piece with a stone or other weight to keep all meat submerged in the brine. Meat should stay here for five or six days, after which it should be overhauled as discussed before. Further overhaulings will be needed in another week and again a couple weeks later. Should the liquid appear stringy or ropy, it should be boiled and strained and the meat repacked after first being washed and the container sterilized. Better still, perhaps, to make a new brine solution. Total curing time in a brine solution is about half as long again as with dry curing.

Brine that collects mold usually imparts a strange flavor. This happens most often with old brine that has bits of meat in suspension. If this happens, destroy the brine and start over again.

The kind of container you use for brine curing is open to some debate. Best advice is never to use a metal one, for metal corrodes when in contact with salt. And if, contrary to advice of some, you wish to use a wooden barrel or box, be certain it is not of soft wood or some other kind of wood with strong odors that would cause your meats to be tainted with an unpleasant flavor. We recommend earthenware crocks.

Earthenware crocks for curing meat come in various sizes.
Figure 4-3

Pumping

If you are using the brine, or sweet pickle, method, you may want to consider "pumping" your meat, especially the larger pieces, before it is put into the containers to cure. Pumping is simply injecting the liquid brine into the meat with a large needle much like a large hypodermic needle with several holes in it. The pump usually holds 4-5 ounces of brine; and, when filled, the needle is inserted deep into the meat and pumped, especially in the bone and joint areas where meat is apt to spoil first, and in the middle of the meat where curing would otherwise happen last. This has the advantage of making certain that the interior starts its cure at the same time the outer parts do, and it also assures that negative enzyme and bacterial action will be stopped sooner than would be possible without pumping. Be sure the pump and needle are sterilized and that the needle never touches other objects while being used to pump the meat. The pump and needle should be completely filled with the brine solution; otherwise air pockets

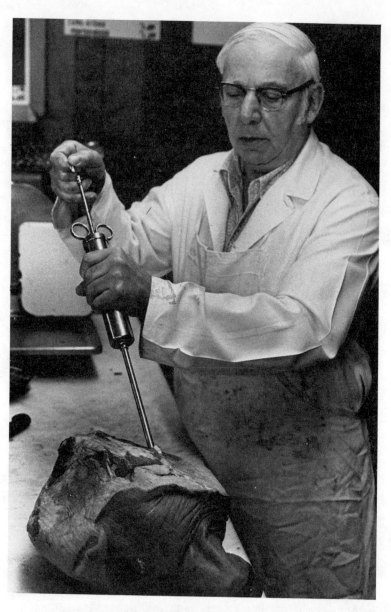

Pumping brine into the ham with brining pump
Figure 4-4

could be injected into the meat along with air impurities which would cause spoilage. Usually about one and a half ounces of brine are adequate for each pound of meat. Should brine start to escape from the holes as the needle is withdrawn, the opening should be squeezed tight and held thus for a few seconds, after which drainage will stop. Pumping doubtless will give a more even cure and a quicker cure providing the brine is injected evenly and thoroughly into the meat. But the big advantage is that it will get the salt solution to the bone and the deep interior much quicker than normal immersion would allow, thus assuring that bacterial action is stopped.

So many things that involve food are debatable. Pumping is one of those. You will find that some claim that meat in a dry cure should never be pumped; it is only for meat in a brine cure. Others disagree with equal fervor. The best answer is to try it and see if you like the results; if not, use the dry cure straight.

Drying and Wrapping

If cured meat is to be stored for any length of time, individual pieces should be wrapped in cheesecloth or muslin after they have been hung up and dried. You might wish to sprinkle them first with spices on the outside to improve their flavor during storage time. Then the pieces should be wrapped tightly in heavy paper and seams sealed with sealing tape. And each individual piece should be wrapped yet again in heavy wrapping paper or in another cloth bag; then hung in a cool, dry place until needed. Be sure that no strings directly connected to the meat are left to protrude outside; else this will provide a direct route for insects to invade the meat. When stored, individual packages of meat should not touch each other; so be sure that air can circulate freely around each piece to keep it cool and dry. Neither should sunlight be allowed to contact the packages, for even though it might not penetrate the wrappings directly, it could still cause meat to lose some of its color. And finally, be certain it is well protected from flies and other insects; this will probably require some sort of screening for the windows; and the finer the mesh the better, for many insects are much, much smaller than the common housefly.

And just to be dead sure that nothing gets into the cured (and smoked) meat, you may wish to paint the outside of the wrapping with what is called a yellow wash. The recipe calls for stirring about six ounces of flour in a half pail of water until all the lumps are out; then dissolving one and a quarter ounces of yellow ocher (which you can order from the drugstore) in a quart of water and adding it to the solution in the pail together with an ounce of dry glue. This should be brought to a boil, at which time you will add three pounds of barium sulphate (also order from the drugstore) slowly while stirring everything. When cool, it may be brushed over the meat wrappings. This recipe is good for a hundred pounds of meat.

Of course, if meat is to be smoked, it would not be wrapped until after smoking is completed.

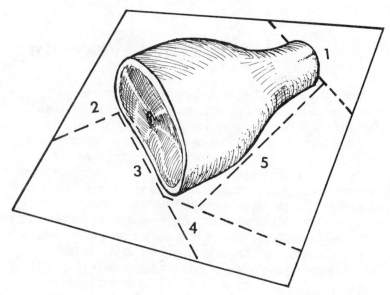

How to wrap a ham. Broken lines show where to fold the paper; numbers show order in which to make folds.

Figure 4-5

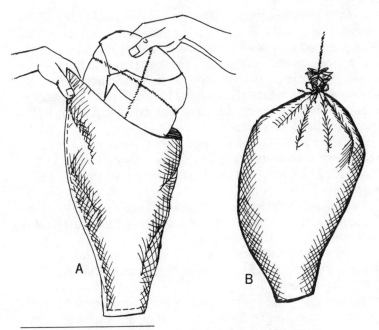

A

B

The above taken from page 6 of USDA Home and Garden Bulletin No. 109 as revised April 1974.

Wrapping a ham for storage: (A) Placing wrapped ham in a closely woven cloth sack. (B) Sacked ham ready for hanging in storeroom.

Figure 4-6

Cured meat that has been properly wrapped will last for many months, often considerably over a year.

The Morton Salt Company of Chicago markets three prepared curing products which can be especially useful to the home processor who wishes to use ingredients already mixed in proper proportions. One product, **Morton Sugar Cure™**, which is a combination of salt, sugar, saltpeter, sodium nitrite, black and red pepper and a combination of spices, comes either with or without smoke flavor, the former allowing one to enjoy the benefits of smoke without having to do the actual smoking. Morton Sugar Cure™ is recommended for applying to the outside of meat being cured. **Morton Tender Quick®** is a combination of salt and other curing ingredients especially recommended for making sweet pickle brines and for pumping. These products also make it easy for the housewife to cure small pieces of meat even in the refrigerator. In addition, Morton markets a special seasoning for meat, poultry, and sausage. Chapter 12 includes some Morton recipes using its prepared curing products.

In the spring of 1974 the United States Department of Agriculture revised its Home and Garden Bulletin No. 109, "Protecting Home-cured Meat from Insects," superseding all previous editions of it.

The following information summarizes the new edition of the Bulletin and should be a guide for protecting home-cured meat products.

Insects that attack home-cured meats are: the cheese skipper, the red-legged ham bettle, the larder beetle, and mites. (See Figure 4-8)

The skipper (which gets its name from the jumping habit of the larvae) bores into cheese and cured meat, resulting in rot and slime where infested. The larvae are yellowish and about a third of an inch long when full grown. The adult skipper that lays the eggs is a two-winged fly about an eighth of an inch long.

Mites feed on the surface of cured meat, and the affected parts become powdery. They are whitish and about one-thirty-second of an inch long when full grown. They crawl instead of fly, and are sometimes borne from place to place by other insects.

The red-legged ham beetle and its larvae attack meat, boring through it and causing it to rot. Larvae are purplish and about one-third inch long. The adults are about one-fourth inch long, a brilliant, greenish blue, with red legs and red at the base of their antennae. They feed on the surface of the meat.

The larder beetle is dark brown with a yellowish band across its back. It is one-third of an inch long. Its larvae feed on or slightly below the surface of the cured meat, but their feeding does not rot the meat. Larvae are fuzzy, brownish, and about one-third inch long when full grown.

What should be done about controlling them?

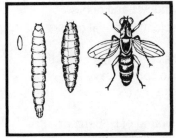

Cheese skipper

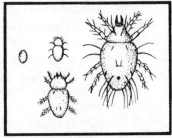

Mite

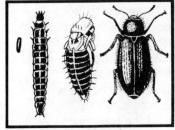

Ham beetle

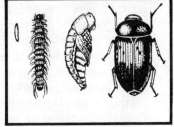

Larder beetle

Above taken from page 3 of USDA Home and Garden Bulletin No. 109 as revised April 1974.

Four Insects That Attack Home-cured Meats
Figure 4-7

1 **Slaughter animals and cure meat during cold weather** when insects and mites are inactive. Be sure hams are sufficiently cured to withstand storage at normal air temperature.
2 **Clean your storeroom** before insects and mites become active. Sweep out your storeroom and scrub it thoroughly with hot soapy water before you store meat in it. Give special attention to cracks in shelves, walls, and floors. Insects and mites feed and breed on grease and tiny scraps of meat lodged in cracks. Seal cracks with putty or plastic wood after you clean them.
3 **Keep pests out.** Flies, ants, and other insects can carry mites into your storeroom around doors and windows. See that doors and windows fit tightly,

Install 30-mesh screens on windows and doors.

4 **Apply insecticides.** After you clean and seal cracks in the storeroom, apply a surface spray to the floor, walls, and other surfaces that do not come in contact with the meat. Surface sprays leave a deposit (thin layer of insecticide), which kills insects that crawl over it.

To make the spray, mix 1 pound of 50-percent methoxychlor wettable powder with each 2½ gallons of water. Apply the spray with a household hand sprayer that delivers a continuous coarse spray. Keep the solution well stirred so the powder will not settle to the bottom of your sprayer.

Wettable-powder sprays leave a powdery deposit on most surfaces. (If a visible deposit is objectionable, use an emulsifiable concentrate of methoxychlor. When diluting the concentrate, follow instructions on the label of the container; add the smallest amount of water recommended.)

Methoxychlor leaves a surface deposit that controls houseflies and other insects of cured meat except mites. Since mites feed on the surface of meat, they can be brushed off and destroyed.

Before meat is put back into the storeroom, apply a spray of synergized pyrethrins to the floor, walls, and other surfaces on which houseflies and other pests are likely to crawl. Use a spray of synergized pyrethrins that contains 0.1 to 0.2 percent pyrethrins and 1 to 2 percent of synergist. (A synergist increases the effectiveness of pyrethrins. Some of the synergists are piperonyl butoxide, sulfoxide, MGK 264, and propyl isome.) Apply the spray with a household hand sprayer that delivers a continuous coarse spray. Do not get the spray on the meat. After the spray dries, you can safely put the meat back into the storeroom.

Consider the following important:

1 **Do not spray the storeroom with insecticides** when it is stocked with meat.
2 **Recommended insecticides may be applied** while meat is in the storeroom if applied with a paintbrush, but only to surfaces that do not come in contact with meat. Treat the surfaces once every 3 months during warm weather if methoxychlor is used. Treatments of pyrethrins may be needed every 30 to 45 days.
3 **Insecticides used improperly can be injurious** to man and animals. Use them only when needed and handle them with care. Follow instructions and heed all precautions on the labels.
4 **Some insecticide compounds contain borax.** Do not use borax in meat storerooms or on meat.

How to protect hams. Bulletin 109 recommends two ways of protecting hams:

1 **By embedding.**
   Get a carton or box that will allow 3 or 4 inches on all sides of the ham you want to embed. Put a 3- or 4-inch layer of cottonseed hulls in the container. Place the ham on the hulls and surround it with more hulls. Inspect the ham about once a month to be sure that it is keeping well. If the hulls become infested with grain beetles, remove the hulls and replace them with new ones.
   Another way to embed hams is simply to bury them in a bin of oats or other grain.
2 **By wrapping and hanging.**
   Wrap each ham separately, and see that it is free of insects before you wrap it. Lay the ham on heavy wrapping paper. Remove the string used to hang the ham for smoking or place it inside the wrapper. Fold the paper as shown in Figure 4-5. Place the wrapped ham in a closely woven cloth sack. Keep the sack free from grease. Check the

bag for holes through which insects might enter.

Loop the top of the sack and tie it tightly with string or single strand rustproof wire. Use the string or wire to hang the ham in the storeroom. Hang hams so they do not touch each other; hang them where rats cannot reach them.

Inspect hams at least once a month. Replace wrapping if it is spotted with grease or if it has holes in it.

Stored meat should be kept cool. The best temperature is between 55° and 60°F. Higher temperatures favor the development of insects.

What to do with infested meat? If meat becomes infested in spite of your preventive measures, remove it from the storeroom and trim out infested parts. Cut deep enough to remove larvae that may have traveled into the meat along the bone or through layers of fat. The uninfested part of the meat is safe to eat, but should be used promptly. Protect the exposed lean or trimmed meat by greasing it with salad oil or melted fat to delay molding or drying.

Smoking: Bringing Out Flavor

Smoking is another activity where one may experiment and bring forth tantalizing flavors that can become hallmarks of a good smoker, and experimentation may help you develop a perfect one that is truly "yours."

The main advantages of smoking are to impart flavor to the meat, to drive out any remaining moisture, and to give a favorable color to the exterior of the meat. The amount of smoking, the kinds of chips used for fuel, and the type of cure preceding smoking (sugar, honey, maple, etc.) will bring forth that particular flavor you want. Such smoking should be "cold smoking" (unless otherwise indicated), for we are not trying to cook meat; it will be cooked later when needed for consumption.

The next chapter describes how to build a smokehouse, and the success of your smoked meat to a large extent will also depend on how well you construct the smokehouse.

Hints

Some of the following hints should help you make it easy to cure meat; others are good to know if you are trying to improve your expertise in producing top quality cures:

1 **Be your own judge of what is good,** how salty meat should be, what flavors you wish to impart to the cure. While we give the standard ingredients for cures, don't be afraid to experiment with your own mixtures, but always be sure you use an adequate amount of salt, to control bacteria and enzymes.

2 **Keep records of what you do,** how you make your dry and sweet pickle cures so you may duplicate them if good or alter them if you wish to emphasize some particular flavor in the future.

3 **Do not freeze uncooked cured meats,** for they will lose much of their cured traits, appearance, and goodness when frozen and being thawed. It is okay to freeze cooked cured meats, and to freeze fresh meat until you are ready to thaw and cure it.

4 **Cured meat will keep for many months** providing:
   You use top quality meat to begin with
   You observe sanitary precautions at all times
   You take no short-cuts to be certain that the salt cure reaches the innermost parts of the meat
   You exercise care in wrapping and storing the cured meat

5 **It is best not to cure meats from different animals together** in a common container, for flavors from one kind of meat tend to invade another with disappointing results.

6 **Remember to pump brine well into the interior of the meat pieces,** if you decide to pump, and especially right up to and around the bones and joints; this is where meat spoils first and fast.
7 **Should you encounter freezing weather** while curing, and should meat freeze, stop the timing and do not continue to count curing time until all meat is thawed.
8 **If you can't keep meat between 38°F and 40°F** while curing, or if you cannot chill it properly immediately following slaughter, do your butchering and processing in the winter when cold weather will provide the lower temperatures you need. Otherwise you may be courting disaster. Remember that lower than 38°F slows the curing process, and higher than 40°F can increase the danger of spoilage.
9 **A brine cure will usually result in a milder flavor** than a dry cure.
10 **Meats that have been frozen do not cure so satisfactorily** as those that have not been frozen.

Later chapters will describe cures for specific meats, for poultry, and for fish; and Chapter 12 contains recipes you may wish to try.

5
HOW TO BUILD A
SMOKEHOUSE AND
DO IT YOURSELF

We frequently hear references to **cold smoking** and to **hot smoking**.

Cold smoking refers to a slow, smouldering smoke that seldom gets above 70° - 90°F. This is the kind of smoke one uses when hams and bacons are smoked. Meat is never cooked during cold smoking because the smoke never becomes hot enough.

Hot smoking is nothing more than cooking with a very hot smoke. Of course if anything is cooked, it has to be consumed, canned, or frozen immediately afterward; meat that has been hot smoked cannot be wrapped and stored as it can if it has undergone a slow, smouldering smoke.

In this book we are concerned with cold smoking. Nevertheless there are times when a recipe will call for smoke that is hotter than the 90°F mentioned above. Even though these instances are few, the temperature called for will not be hot enough to cook the meat.

Basic Units
of a Smokehouse

An efficient smokehouse is very simple and inexpensive to build. It may be constructed from so many different materials that one's imagination is the only limiting factor. While some metal smokehouses are available from hardware stores and mail order outlets, for the most part these are too small for the purpose of smoking large pieces of meat; their use is better reserved for those who wish to prepare hot smoked food for individual meals and for parties.

For cold smoking one needs to provide for the following when building one's smokehouse: 1 **A fire pit.** 2 **A smoke chamber where the meat is actually smoked.** 3 **A smoke tunnel** to direct the smoke from the fire pit to the smoke chamber. With these three units in mind, it takes but little imagination to find material around the house that can be used to build a successful smokehouse.

The Fire Pit

The fire pit should be set into the ground two to two-and-a-half feet deep. This could be an old kettle, a simple box, or other type of enclosure in which a fire may be built. A simple hole in the ground might well do, too; however it would be best to line it with rocks. But the pit must have a top, if only a board across; for this will act as a damper to regulate the draft and to control the amount of fire in the pit. A metal cover would be ideal, be it the top of an old metal drum or a piece of sheet metal. (See Figure 5-1)

The Smoke Chamber

This is the unit in which the meat is actually smoked. Therefore it should be large enough to accommodate the amount of meat being processed. Again, we could use an old metal drum, a wooden box, a metal cabinet, or what have you. And be certain it is clean; time spent in scrubbing it to remove all dirt and anything that could conceivably impart an unwanted flavor to the meat will be time well spent. And there should be

The Fire Pit
Figure 5-1

no paint or fresh painted enamel on the smoke chamber interior to cause unpleasant odors and tastes and to give off chemical poisons. Wash with a mild detergent; then rinse with pure water and let it dry in the air until ready for use.

Not only does the smoke chamber contain smoke to surround the meat, it also must have a method to control the escape of smoke in order that fresh smoke will constantly be rising around and past the meat. So there must be a top to the smoke chamber that can be opened and closed in a controlled way to act as a damper for the draft. This can be improvised from boards, the top of a metal drum, a piece of sheet metal, or from a dozen other things found around the house or farm.

Some people use wooden barrels for smoke chambers; but since the staves tend to shrink under even mild heat, smoke can escape from the sides leaving an insufficient amount in the chamber to process the meat. Such escape through the sides could also result in uneven smoking. A metal drum would be

The Smoke Chamber
Figure 5-2

more satisfactory or a box that would not shrink - preferably
made from long-seasoned hardwood. (See Figure 5-2)

The smoke chamber should have provisions for suspending
the meat while being smoked; crosspieces from branches,
dowels, or similar would be fine to suspend across the top of
the chamber. Twine, wire, S-hooks, or similar means may be
used to suspend the meat from these crosspieces. One might
prefer to use wire mesh shelves (especially for small pieces of
meat), in which case shelf brackets would have to be secured to
the interior sides of the chamber. If so, they should be installed
to provide easy removal for cleaning. The best mesh would be
stainless steel; but in any event stay away from galvanized
wire, brass, or copper inasmuch as these can give off oxides or
chemicals that are injurious to the meat and to the one who
consumes it.

Some people have been very successful using old
refrigerators for smoke chambers. These have the advantage of

having removable shelves built into them. They can easily have a hole cut in the top for the smoke escape and one in the bottom for the smoke tunnel connection. But if you use a refrigerator, be careful that it is padlocked when unattended; far too many children have met fatal ends by inadvertently closing the door and locking themselves inside old refrigerators while playing. (See Figure 5-3)

The base of the smoke chamber should ideally be slightly up-hill from the top of the fire pit and about ten feet away. This will facilitate draft from the fire pit to the smoke chamber and make construction of the smoke tunnel more simple.

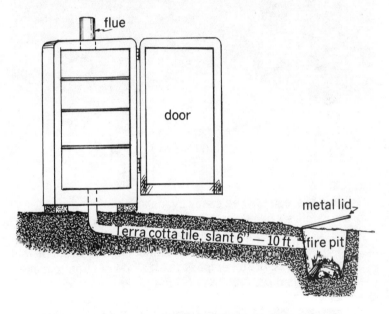

Smokehouse Created From An Old Refrigerator
Figure 5-3

The Smoke Tunnel

Now that we have provided for the smoke pit and the smoke chamber, our next job is to connect the two so that smoke will leave the pit and surround the meat in the smoke chamber before it escapes through the outlet at its top (Figure 5-4).

The Smoke Tunnel
Figure 5-4

All this is accomplished easily by making a hole, approximately six inches in diameter, in the side of the smoke pit about one foot from the top, making a similar hole in the bottom of the smoke chamber, and connecting the two. For this we can use a piece of stovepipe with an elbow section to make the connections directly to the hole in the bottom of the chamber.

Since the smoke pit is below ground level, and since the chamber is set on ground level, the smoke tunnel will be entirely beneath the surface of the ground; in other words, buried. This is exactly what we want, for it will keep the smoke cool; furthermore since the pit and the chamber are at different levels, the smoke tunnel is on an incline, and this is what we want, too, for it helps provide a draft for the smoke and fire.

It might be simpler just to dig a trench from the pit to the chamber, using elbow stovepipe connections to the tunnel as mentioned above, cover the trench with a board, and then cover the board with dirt to ground level.

But checking for available supplies around the house will make it easy to find many ways to build a simple smoke tunnel that will cool the smoke and provide a good draft.

Important Considerations

However you finally decide to make your smokehouse, be sure it provides the following:

> **Easy cleaning.** Periodically the smoke chamber and its shelves or racks should be scrubbed and cleaned to remove stale odors, dirt accumulations, and grime.
>
> **Easy access** to putting meat in for smoking and taking it out when done.
>
> **Protection from flies** and other insects. Use screening or have some type of cover to put over the smoke chamber when it is not actually in use. Preferably use something that will allow air to circulate around and in it.
>
> **Protection from animals.** It is easy to imagine the inquisitive raccoon getting into the smoke chamber, perhaps even via the fire pit and smoke tunnel. Percautions should be taken to avoid this.

The Fire

What about the fire? Remember it is smoke that we are after, and not hot smoke. We really need just a low, and steady fire that will produce smoke. Some people prefer to start it with a charcoal base and add the proper wood to it; others prefer an electric hot-plate (which usually has the advantage of being regulated easily, or even thermostatically controlled) and putting the wood chips in a pan on the hot-plate to smoulder and create smoke. Purists denounce charcoal and petro-chemicals for starting the fire, but this is something that each person will have to work out for himself.

Occasionally one sees a smokehouse with a fire pit directly under the smoke chamber. This may be quite all right for hot smoking and actually cooking in a smoke chamber, but it should be avoided if at all possible for cold smoking. Such fire pits are far too difficult to regulate and control; furthermore if the heat from the smoke causes the meat to drip, fat can run down on the fire causing flare-ups and intense heat that can harm the meat or even partially cook it.

Fuel

Inasmuch as smoking has two purposes -- preserving the meat and imparting a flavor -- it is important that you use the kind of wood that appeals most to your individual taste. If you are a beginner, some experimentation will be necessary and fun. USE ONLY HARDWOOD; that means wood from trees that shed their leaves in the winter: maple, birch, apple, hickory, chestnut, ash, etc. Wood from the softwood trees (pines, spruce, hemlock, balsam, cedar, and other such trees that do not shed their needles in the winter) is not suitable at all, for it gives off a pitch when burned that not only imparts a bad taste to the meat but also can coat the meat with a film that impedes preservation.

Another type of fuel that has been successfully used for years, especially in New England, has been dried corn cobs. And one young woman whom we recently met was bragging about the wonderful flavor she got when using butternuts in the husk for fuel.

Whether hardwood or corn cobs, they should be cut into small bits, or shavings, or reduced to sawdust, if possible, to provide fuel to generate smoke. If the fuel burns too fast, dampen it down with water. Or use green twigs or green leaves from these hardwood trees to smoulder and generate smoke.

If you have problems finding hardwood shavings, sawdust, or chips, check with the local lumber yard or consult the ads in the telephone directory. For special flavors, for instance hickory, it is possible to order from companies specializing in shavings or chips of hickory or other woods for the very purpose of smoking. The following are a couple such sources:

Gander Mountain, Inc.
P.O. Box 248
Wilmot, Wisconsin 53129

Brenner Sawdust Company
26 Kent Street
Brooklyn, New York 11222

Distribution of Smoke

It is important that meat in the chamber be entirely exposed to the smoke; otherwise the flavor will not be properly distributed, the meat will not be smoked for preservation, and the color of the meat will vary. Therefore be dead certain that no meat touches other pieces of meat nor touches the sides of the smoke chamber. Furthermore, it may be necessary to build a baffle to distribute smoke evenly throughout the chamber if the draft is such that it does not allow this to happen. This is easily done. The cover of a metal drum or a board, for instance, cut to fit inside the smoke chamber below the level of the meat, can easily be punched with small holes evenly dispersed over the surface of it. Smoke will tend to build up against the under surface of the cover, and the draft will take it on up through the holes, more evenly dispersing the smoke than would be the case if it came up directly from the smoke tunnel via the main draft. And of course it will be necessary to provide for some brackets to hold the baffle in place inside the smoke chamber.

Illustrations of a Smokehouse

Experiment with a simple smokehouse. Learn all you can about fuel, drafts, smoke flavor, and all that goes into bringing forth a piece of meat, beautifully smoked, succulent, and at the peak of flavor. Don't invest in permanent equipment until you are sure you know precisely what you want for a permanent installation, if indeed you do require a permanent smokehouse.

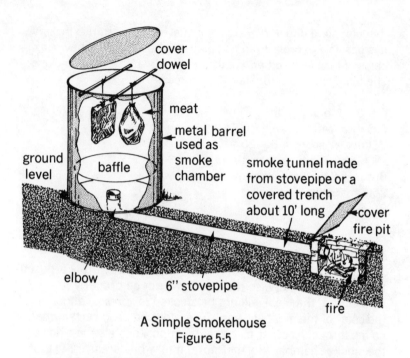

cover
dowel
meat
metal barrel used as smoke chamber
ground level
baffle
smoke tunnel made from stovepipe or a covered trench about 10' long
cover
fire pit
elbow
6" stovepipe
fire

A Simple Smokehouse
Figure 5-5

The above sketch (Figure 5-5) will show you what we have been talking about. But again, the variations are legion. And should you decide that you need something more elaborate and more permanent, we suggest that you write to the Government Printing Office in Washington, D.C. for a copy of Farmers' Bulletin No. 2138 put out by the Department of Agriculture; page 43 of the bulletin will provide you with more information.

6
BEEF AND VEAL

No attempt will be made here to describe how to cut up a beef carcass or how to take the necessary sanitary precautions when cutting up meat. If you prefer to slaughter rather than having it done in an approved slaughterhouse, it is suggested that you read Farmers' Bulletin No. 2209 put out by the United States Department of Agriculture titled "Slaughtering, Cutting and Processing Beef on the Farm" for instructions unless you already know how to do it. Charts put out by the National Life Stock and Meat Board in Chicago will also prove helpful. Instructions for the sanitary handling of meat were adequately covered in the chapter on canning; so are not repeated here.

Should you decide to purchase your beef carcass from a commercial slaughterhouse where it will have been properly chilled and aged waiting your cutting, try to find a slaughterhouse that is under federal inspection and look for a grading stamp that indicates top quality. The younger the beef at the time of slaughter, the whiter and more flexible the breastbone will be. Older animals tend to have darker breastbones, which are stiff and lack flexibility.

Condition of Beef Before Slaughter

We asked a friend in a large slaughterhouse what one factor in his opinion contributes the most to making meat tender. His reply was quick: "The condition of the animal," he said.

People who work in slaughter and packing houses know that if one wants top quality meat, one has to start with top quality animals. Slaughtering and processing cannot impart to meat quality that is not already there.

They know equally well that the way an animal is handled before slaughter is also most important.

So, if you want your beef to be in as top condition as possible start feeding it a half bag of grain a week for about three months preceding slaughter and get it fattened up. A fat beef is better than a lean one, and it will be more tender providing the meat is marbelized throughout with fine streaks of fat. Marbelized meat reduces the chances of drying out and of freezer burn.

All animals should be calm before slaughter; otherwise the meat becomes warmer than normal, requiring more time to chill, and meat may even take on a sour taint if it is abnormally warm when the animal is killed. Slaughter should be quick and should not cause the animal to become excited.

It is a good idea to cut off all food for 24 hours prior to slaughter but to give the animal plenty of fresh water during this period.

THE PRIMARY CUTS OF BEEF

For means of identification, Figure 6-1 illustrating the primary cuts of beef will be helpful. Since this is a book on processing (canning, freezing, curing, and smoking to preserve and store meat for future consumption), we shall not be concerned with the disposition of animal wastes (bones, blood, waste fats, and other products which do have uses although not for usual human consumption).

The following list shows the uses of the primary cuts of beef.

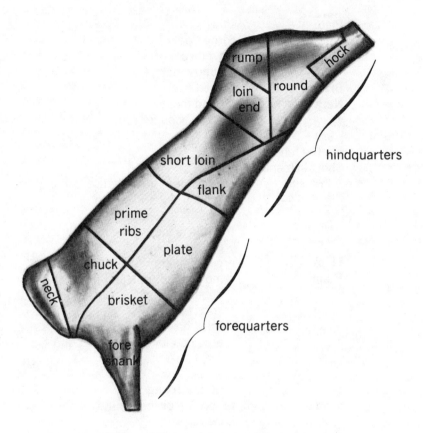

Primary Cuts of Beef
Figure 6-1

Do not be misled into thinking that there are not other uses for some of the primary cuts, but these are the ones that are more or less standard.

From the forequarters:

Chuck...	pot roasts	**Foreshank**...	stew meat
	some steaks		soup bone
	corned beef		ground meat
	short ribs		
	stew meat	**Prime ribs**...	standing rib roasts
	ground meat		rib steaks

Plate............ short ribs
corned beef
stew meat
ground meat
Brisket.......... corned beef
Neck............ ground meat
use the bone for soup

From the hindquarters:
Short loin and
loin end .... steaks: club, porterhouse, T-bone,
tenderloin, and sirloin
roasts
trimmings for ground meat or for
braising
Flank .... ground meat or flank steak
Rump .... remove bone, roll, and tie for
boneless roasts
corned beef
Round .... steaks; however the last six inches
are good for stew and ground
meat
roasts
good for drying
Hind shank ...... for boiling or for ground meat
bone for soup
Kidney .... use fresh or for sausage
Tongue.......... cure and smoke
Heart .... use fresh or for sausage
Liver............ use fresh or for sausage
Tripe............ pickled tripe

Yield

Of course the dressed carcass is going to weigh considerably
less than the animal's live weight because of the removal of
wastes: hide, blood, water, and some bones. Table 6-1
shows what you may expect from the dressed carcass of an
animal weighing 750 pounds before slaughter:

TABLE 6-1*

Trimmed quarters	Live weight (percent)	Carcass weight (percent)	Yield (pounds)
Hindquarters	27.5	49.0	206
Forequarters	28.5	51.0	214
Total	56.0	100.0	420

And the approximate yield of trimmed beef cuts from the dressed forequarters and hindquarters are as follows:**

Trimmed cuts	Live weight (percent)	Carcass weight (percent)	Yield (pounds)
Steaks and oven roasts	23.0	41.0	172
Pot roasts	11.5	20.0	84
Stew and ground meats	11.5	20.0	84
Fat trim and bone	10.0	19.0	80
Total	56.0	100.0	420

---

*From USDA Farmers' Bulletin No. 2209
**Ibid

Don't Waste Meat

There is a tendency for many to throw out valuable parts of the beef carcass as waste or to use it for dog and cat food. Many commercial slaughterhouses automatically segregate cuts that would require extra time to cut up and sell them to the processors of dog and cat food; and these processors often pay very high prices for these parts. But on the farm it would be well to give thought to the use of such pieces of meat for human consumption. Outside of the normal wastes, there is hardly anything in the beef carcass that cannot be used for human consumption; almost anything can be used in ground meat and mixed with pork for sausage.

As many as fifteen pounds of excellent meat may be found in the head of a beef; yet so many slaughterhouses toss the heads into the waste pile or sell to processors of pet foods. But tongues are excellent for smoking, lips for hamburg, brains for fresh meat, cheeks for hamburg or sausage. The pancreas (sweetbread) is considered a delicacy by many a gourmet, and a professional butcher with over forty-five years' experience has remarked that a cow's udder has some of the most delicate meat he has ever tasted; he pointed out that it is not uncommon for some butcher shops in the city to sell this as "veal chops" to unsuspecting customers, and they love it. The heart, liver, and kidneys are among the most highly nutritional parts of the beef and should never be thrown out. The inner lining of the stomach makes excellent tripe and is of high food value.

So before you toss these cuts and organs to the dogs and cats, stop and consider eating or processing them for later household use. And incidently you will be saving on your meat bill by doing so.

In any event, the beef carcass should be chilled for at least five days before being cut up. The temperature should be as close to 32°F as possible without freezing. (We find that many managers of slaughterhouses try to hold the temperature at a steady 34°F.) Some people prefer to age their beef beyond this period as a sort of ripening process during which time the meat will become somewhat darker in color. This aging process may be continued for as much as two to three weeks in some instances, and during this period great care must be taken to guard against taint, foul odor, or decay that would indicate spoilage is setting in. If you plan to age the carcass of your beef past the normal chilling period, remember that the leaner the beef, the shorter should be the aging period.

Canning

Review Chapter 2, remembering that meat must be canned with the use of a pressure canner in order that a temperature of 240°F may be reached and maintained during the canning process. Other points to remember in connection with canning meat are:

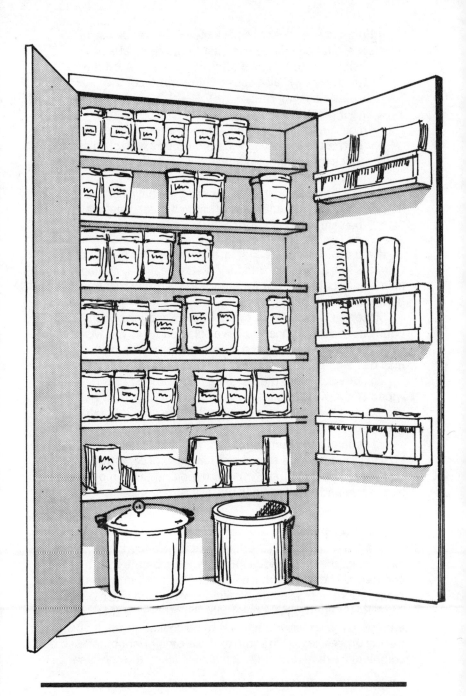

Either raw pack or hot pack methods may be used.

Excess fat should be trimmed from the meat since fat will often turn rancid after canning and spoil the meat. Fat will also cause deterioration of the rubber sealing rings.

Either plain tin cans or glass jars may be used for containers. If the latter, you will save yourself a lot of trouble if you use wide-mouth jars with straight sides (no shoulders); meat will be easier to pack and easier to remove.

Since aging does little to enhance the flavor or the permanent tenderness of canned meat, beef may be canned soon after chilling.

If you desire large, tender cuts, it is best to select pieces from the loin as well as cuts for roasts, steaks, and chops. The less tender cuts are best for stew meat, ground meat, and the bony pieces for soups.

Since you will not want to waste cans and jars, you should bone out the meat once you have selected what you wish to can. The bones may be used to simmer for broth, or the marrow may be used to add to soups.

Do not wash meat that is going to be canned, but it may be wiped clean with a damp cloth; and you will not then risk the possibility of washing away a considerable amount of its goodness.

To estimate the number of cans or jars needed, plan on a quart container or its equivalent for each three to three and a half pounds of fresh, untrimmed round and the same for each five to five and a half pounds of fresh, untrimmed rump.

Preparation of Meat

Meat should be cut length-wise of its grain into pieces one to two inches thick. Individual pieces should be the length of the container. The less tender parts should be cut into small pieces. Containers should be filled to within one inch of their tops. Remember to pack meat loosely; otherwise there could be a tendency for interior parts not to be cooked through enough during processing. Also some of the air might not otherwise be completely exhausted. Instructions for filling the containers, which will follow, suggest adding salt before processing; this, however, is not necessary if you prefer to salt to taste when preparing meat for the table.

Preparation of Broth

Bony pieces with meat are excellent for making broth. Put them in a saucepan, cover with water, and let simmer. When meat is tender, skim off the fat, and add the broth to the containers instead of merely adding boiling water. Simmer at 185°F or above.

Processing Time

Once the pressure in your canner has reached 10 to 15 pounds, depending on altitude (240°F), regulate the source of heat so it will remain steady, and start counting time. A general rule is that pint jars or cans containing large pieces of meat should process for 75 minutes, quart-sized jars and cans for 90 minutes. Then the pressure canner should be taken off from the heat, cooled, and the containers removed and cooled as described in Chapter 2.

Hot Pack/Raw Pack

The processing of meat in glass jars differs somewhat from meat in metal cans. Instructions for cut-up meat differ from ground meat, sausage, and cured meat; and hot packing meat differs from the raw pack method. Therefore we shall describe below some of these variables. Refer to altitude listing on p. 16 for proper pressure.

Directions for cut-up meat.
Hot Pack. Put meat in large shallow pan; add just enough water to keep from sticking. Cover pan. Precook meat slowly until medium done. Stir occasionally, so meat heats evenly.

1   In glass jars. Pack hot meat loosely. Leave 1 inch of space at top of jars. Add salt if desired: ½ teaspoon

to pints or 1 teaspoon to quarts. Cover meat with boiling meat juice, adding boiling water if needed. Leave 1 inch of space at top of jars. Adjust lids. Process in a pressure canner at 10 to 15 pounds pressure (240°F).

Pint jars .... 75 minutes
Quart jars .... 90 minutes

2 In tin cans. Pack hot meat loosely. Leave ½ inch of space above meat. Add salt if desired: ½ teaspoon to No. 2 cans or ¾ teaspoon to No. 2½ cans. Fill cans to top with boiling meat juice, adding boiling water if needed. Seal. Process in a pressure canner at 10 to 15 pounds pressure (240°F).

No. 2 cans .... 65 minutes
No. 2½ cans .... 90 minutes

Raw Pack. Cut up meat. Pack containers loosely with raw, lean meat.

1 In glass jars. Leave 1 inch of space above meat. To exhaust air, cook raw meat in jars at slow boil to 170°F or until medium done (about 75 minutes). Add salt if desired: ½ teaspoon per pint or 1 teaspoon per quart. Adjust lids. Process in a pressure canner at 10 to 15 pounds pressure (240°F).

Pint jars .... 75 minutes
Quart jars .... 90 minutes

2 In tin cans. Pack cans to top. To exhaust air, cook raw meat in cans at slow boil to 170°F or until medium done (about 50 minutes). Press meat down ½ inch below rim, and add boiling water to fill to top, if needed. Add salt if desired: ½ teaspoon to No. 2 cans or ¾ teaspoon to No. 2½ cans. Seal cans. Process in a pressure canner at 10 to 15 pounds pressure (240°F).

No. 2 cans .... 65 minutes
No. 2½ cans .... 90 minutes

Directions for ground meat. For grinding, start with fresh clean, cold meat. Use small pieces of meat from less tender cuts. Do not mix leftover scraps with fresh meat. Don't use lumps of fat. If desired, add 1 teaspoon of salt per pound of ground meat. Mix well.

Hot Pack. Shape ground meat into fairly thin patties that can be packed into jars or cans without breaking. Precook patties in slow oven (325° F) until medium done. Skim fat off drippings; do not use fat for canning.

1   In glass jars. Pack patties, leaving 1 inch of space above meat. Cover with boiling meat juice to 1 inch of top of jars. Adjust jar lids. Process in a pressure canner at 10 to 15 pounds pressure (240° F).

    Pint jars . . . . 75 minutes
    Quart jars . . . . 90 minutes

2   In tin cans. Pack patties to ½ inch of top of cans. Cover with boiling meat juice to fill cans to top; seal. Process in a pressure canner at 10 to 15 pounds pressure (240° F).

    No. 2 cans . . . . 65 minutes
    No. 2½ cans . . . . 90 minutes

Raw Pack. Raw pack is suitable for tin cans. Ground meat canned in bulk is difficult to get out of jars.

In tin cans. Pack raw ground meat solidly to top of the can. To exhaust air, cook meat at slow boil to 170° F or until medium done (about 75 minutes). Press meat down into cans ½ inch below rim. Seal. Process in a pressure canner at 10 to 15 pounds pressure (240° F).

    No. 2 cans . . . . 100 minutes
    No. 2½ cans . . . . 135 minutes

Directions for sausage.

Hot Pack. Use any tested sausage recipe. Use seasoning sparingly because sausage changes flavor in canning and storage. Measure spices, onion, and garlic carefully. Omit sage - it makes canned sausage bitter. Shape sausage meat into patties. Precook, pack, and process as directed for hot-packed ground meat.

Directions for Corned Beef. Use any tested recipe for corned beef. Wash it. Drain. Cut it into pieces or strips that fit in containers. Cover meat with cold water and bring to a boil. If broth is very salty, drain meat; boil again in fresh water. Pack while hot.

1 In glass jars. Leave 1 inch of space above meat. Cover meat with boiling broth or boiling water. Leave 1 inch of space at top of jars. Adjust lids. Process in a pressure canner at 10 to 15 pounds pressure (240° F).
    Pint jars .... 75 minutes
    Quart jars .... 90 minutes

2 In tin cans. Leave ½ inch of space above meat. Fill cans to top with boiling water or boiling broth. Seal. Process in a pressure canner at 10 to 15 pounds pressure (2140° F).
    No. 2 cans .... 65 minutes
    No. 2½ cans .... 90 minutes

Directions for meat-vegetable stew.
Raw Pack. Meat should be cut into 1½ inch cubes, potatoes in ½ inch cubes, carrots pared or scraped into ½ inch cubes, celery into ¼ inch pieces, and onions peeled and small if whole. Combine ingredients.

1 In glass jars. Fill jars to top with raw meat-vegetable mixture. Add salt if desired: ½ teaspoon per pint or 1 teaspoon per quart. Adjust lids. Process in a pressure canner at 10 to 15 pounds pressure (240° F).
    Pint jars .... 60 minutes
    Quart jars .... 75 minutes

2 In tin cans. Fill cans to top with raw meat-vegetable mixture. Do not add liquid. Add salt if desired: ½ teaspoon to No. 2 cans or 1 teaspoon to

No. 2½ cans. To exhaust air, cook stew at slow boil
to 170° F or until medium done (about 50 minutes).
Seal cans. Process in a pressure canner at 10 to 15
pounds pressure (240° F).

    No. 2 cans .... 40 minutes
    No. 2½ cans .... 45 minutes

Directions for heart and tongue.

Heart: remove thick connective tissue before
         cutting into pieces.
Tongue: drop tongue into boiling water and simmer
         about 45 minutes, or until skin can be
         removed. Then cut into pieces.
Use hot pack for heart and tongue as described for
cut-up meat.

Directions for soup stock. For canning, make meat
stock fairly concentrated. Cover bony pieces of meat
with lightly salted water. Simmer until tender. Skim
off fat. Remove all bones. Leave meat and sediment
in stock. Use hot pack method.

1   In glass jars. Pour boiling soup stock into jars, leaving
    1 inch of space at top. Adjust lids. Process in a
    pressure canner at 10 to 15 pounds pressure (240° F).

        Pint jars .... 20 minutes
        Quart jars .... 25 minutes

2   In tin cans. Fill cans to top with boiling soup stock
    Seal. Process in a pressure canner at 10 to 15
    pounds pressure (240° F).

        No. 2 cans .... 20 minutes
        No. 2½ cans .... 25 minutes

Freezing

Freezing is probably the simplest of all processing methods. Chapter 3 describes in detail the freezing process, and there is no point in repeating much of it now; however it would be a good idea to review that chapter as background before freezing beef. So we'll confine our remarks here to listing some hints and reminders and bits of other information that may prove helpful.

- Once you have selected the cuts you wish to freeze, consider boning them, for cutting the bone out will save freezer space and cost of freezer operation.
- Be sure to leave the metal band on jars of frozen food because the jars are never vacuum-sealed as in canning; accordingly the lids will fall off if the bands are removed.
- Trim off excess fat because fat has a tendency to become rancid when frozen. If food has already been cooked, cool it before freezing so that fat from both broth and gravy may be skimmed off.
- Omit salt when freezing because salt can cause meat to spoil in the freezer.
- All cooked meat should be cooled quickly before freezing.
- Smoked and cured meats lose much of their looks and value when thawed unless they are first cooked prior to freezing.
- Stew meat should be cut into cubes for freezing; cooked meat should be covered with gravy whenever possible.
- Be sure to leave some headroom in rigid containers, for contents will expand when being frozen.
- The more tightly you wrap the meat, the more air will be driven out of the package and the less will be the danger of wrapping potentially harmful organisms that might be in the air.

- Recommendations for maximum storage periods of home-frozen beef*:

  Ground meat ....2-3 months
  Roasts ....8-12 months
  Steaks...........................8-12 months
  Stew meat ....2-3 months

Precooked combination dishes should usually be consumed within 5-6 months.

Frozen meat may be cooked either thawed or before thawing; but if the latter, more time will be required to cook it. If there is ample time to thaw meat before cooking, the results will generally be more satisfactory.

Curing

Chapter 4 provides the background for curing meat. Review it before proceeding further.

The major ways of curing beef are corning and making dried beef. However the recipe for corning may be changed a bit to make the very tasteful pastrami; this requires the addition of special spices and herbs, and pastrami may be smoked, resulting in what is called "beef bacon." Some may recall that when President Eisenhower was ill he was allowed to have beef bacon, and shortly thereafter some of the airlines began serving beef bacon on breakfast flights. And of course beef may also be used in sausage. But since sausage is generally improved by combining beef and pork, the subject of making sausage will be taken up in Chapter 7 when we discuss pork.

If one spends a little time chatting with people who make corned beef and dried beef, one will discover that there are a number of variations to basic recipes; often only subtle ones; in fact variations are rampant for sausages, hams, bacon, and other kinds of cured meats. These variations have frequently been handed down in families from generation to generation

---

*From USDA Home and Garden Bulletin No. 93

until one knows he will be able to obtain his favorite flavor of corned beef from a particular family's recipe and his favorite flavor of dried beef from another. So, no one should feel he has to be bound tightly to any one particular combination of ingredients for curing (and smoking) meats; a little experimenting is good to find a combination that is distinctive and a special favorite; however one should never lose respect for the basic ingredients that are required to preserve meat - salt, sugar, and saltpeter (although saltpeter may be considered by some to be optional).

Preserving in Lard

Although we are not recommending preserving meat in lard, this is a method that has been used often in times past and even up to the present day with fairly successful results. Now that we have refrigerators, freezers, and facilities for easy canning and curing, preserving in lard is seldom done because these other methods are much safer.

Hunters, too, have used this method when others were not convenient.

A sterilized crock is most commonly used, and layers of cooked meat packed into it. Each layer is completely covered with melted lard, and the top layer especially well covered. A double layer of cheese cloth or a layer of muslin or waxed paper is put over the top and held down by a cover or by a plate. As meat is removed to be consumed, care must be taken to see that the remaining meat is well covered with melted lard.

And it is important that the crock be stored in a cool, dry place with temperatures well under 40°F, and that this method not be used for meat being stored for long periods of time.

As already mentioned, we are not recommending this method.

Miscellaneous Information on Beef. Here are a few hints that may save you time and money, yet help you, too, in processing your beef.

- **Fat on the carcasses of Jersey cows is apt to be quite yellow.** This does no harm whatsoever; it is just the natural coloration.

- **Whenever there is bone in meat, there is likely to be fat.** Some of the most tender cuts of meat are those from the bony areas.
- **Contrary to common opinion, bright red meat is not a sign that it is superior** to dark meat. If meat has been properly aged, it will turn a dark red color; such cuts are preferable to others. Purchased meat that is bright red can almost correctly be assumed to have had its color fixed with additives, the only purpose of which is to fool the customer.
- **Dark red meat without fat tends to be tough;** in fact it will be tough even if it is surrounded by fat but without fat running through it. Fat must be marbelized in meat for meat to be tender, i.e. fine streaks of fat throughout.

Veal

Since calves have little fat under their hides, the carcass of veal must be cut and processed as soon as possible to avoid loss of moisture. It should, nevertheless, chill at normal chilling temperatures. Process the meat as soon as the carcass is thoroughly chilled; do not prolong chilling and never age veal.

The USDA recommends that the carcass be cut and processed similar to beef carcass. Some packing houses even so vary the cuts somewhat. We should recall that cuts recommended for corned beef and for dried beef were those having a considerable amount of fat on them; since fat is missing on veal, corned and dried beef made from the veal carcass will not be satisfactory, and the cuts should be used for other purposes.

Veal from young beef cattle is generally considered more satisfactory than veal from other kinds of cattle. Since it has such a small amount of fat on it, it is one of the fastest spoiling meats. Close to one-half the live weight of a veal is lost by the time it is slaughtered and trimmed.

Be especially alert to spoilage of the liver, heart, and sweetbread because there is virtually no fat on them. It is best to freeze or eat them soon after slaughter.

Following is the average freezer storage time for home-frozen veal:

For roasts . . . . .4 to 8 months
For cutlets . . . . .3 to 4 months
For chops . . . . .3 to 4 months

7
PORK

Care of Hogs Before Slaughter

Hogs should be penned individually for at least 24 hours preceding slaughter. During this period they should be denied food, for this fasting period will improve a thorough bleed following slaughter. During the 24-hour period they should be allowed to drink all the water they want. Keep the animals calm and give them no reason to become excited, for excitement will impede bleeding and cause the meat to spoil easily.

We shall now assume that your hog has been slaughtered; also that it has been chilled at a temperature of approximately 32°F, but without freezing, for a couple days. Pork should never be aged beyond normal chilling time since it is a rather perishable meat; so now we shall also assume it has been cut ready for use or for processing.

A Word About Trichinosis

We should take a moment, however, to discuss trichinosis. Hogs are extremely susceptible to trichinae infection if they have been allowed to eat uncooked garbage, raw pork bones, offal, or the raw flesh of other animals that have been infected with trichinae worms. When such infected animals are butchered and their meat is consumed by humans, these trichinae worms will invade their muscles and the blood stream causing severe illness and complications. But the trichinae worms in meat may be killed in one of two ways:

1 By holding the meat at a temperature of **10°F below zero** for a period of forty days, or

2 By cooking the meat until the temperature at the center of each piece (and this means the very center - even the bones) reaches 185°F. Cured hams should be cooked until the center of them reaches 160°F, and tenderized picnics to 170°F. If you do not have a thermometer, be safe by cooking meat thirty minutes to the pound minimum; and even then inspect the center of the meat to be sure it is not red but well cooked. Frozen meats take longer to cook than fresh meats; so act accordingly. The main warning, then, with pork is this: **do not eat pork that is not thoroughly cooked**; sausage, especially, should always be thoroughly cooked through if it is made in the home or purchased from non-federally inspected plants.

Right here it might be well to emphasize again that if your hog has been slaughtered at a commercial slaughterhouse that is under federal inspection, you may assume the hog was healthy and has passed inspection. If, however, the hog is to be slaughtered on the farm, it would be well to have it inspected by a veterinarian before slaughter if you suspect its health and quality. If the veterinarian suspects it also, he will advise having laboratory tests made.

THE PRIMARY CUTS OF PORK

For means of identification, Figure 7-1 illustrates the primary cuts of pork.

The following list shows the uses of the primary cuts of pork. Although there are occasionally other uses for these cuts, these are the ones that have become more or less standard.

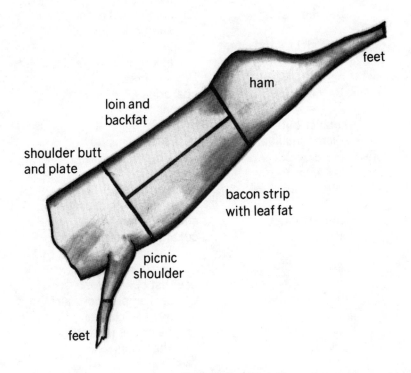

The Primary Cuts of Pork
Figure 7-1

Ham .... fresh ham
curing and smoking

Loin and backfat
   Loin........................... bone out muscle for
                                 canning or for
                                 sausage
roasts, if unboned
chops:
      shoulder end chops
      center chops
      chops from ham end

| | Canadian bacon with a slight cure |
| Backfat .... | for making lard or for salt pork |

Bacon strip with leaf fat
Leaf fat	for making lard or for salt pork
Bacon strip	spareribs
	bacon

Shoulder butt and plate
Picnic shoulder	cure with hams
Plate	for lard or cure as salt pork
Butt	roast or cure with bacon or use with sausage

Picnic shoulder .... cure with ham
Head .... cut and trim jowls; then cure and smoke or use in sausage

use rest of head for cooked products such as head cheese

Feet .... pickle or use in head cheese

Internal products such as liver,
heart, and tongue ...... for cooked products and for sausage

Caul and ruffle fat from
internal organs .... for lard

Yield

It has been estimated* that a hog weighing 225 pounds live will result in a dressed carcass of 176 pounds. Table 7-1 indicates the yield of the various cuts.

From the table it will be seen that approximately 20% of the live weight of a hog is lost in slaughter, and this sometimes

---

*USDA Farmers' Bulletin No. 2138

TABLE 7-1

Cuts	Live weight 225 lbs Percent	Carcass weight 176 lbs Percent	Yield Pounds
Fresh hams, picnic shoulders, bacon, loin, and shoulder butt	50	64	113
Ribs, sausage, feet, and head	15	19	34
Fat from lard	12	15	27
Trim	2	2	2
Total	79	100	176

goes as high as 35% depending, of course, on the quality of the hog.

My good friend the butcher tells me with some slight exaggeration, I am sure, that the only parts of a hog he throws away are the eyeballs! He uses all organs in various cooked products, the tail for stew, and the intestines for sausage casings. Of course his main point is that much of food value is customarily tossed out when indeed it could be used for food to mark up further savings on the food dollar.

Canning

As this book says so many times, meat must be canned with a temperature of 240°F, and the only safe way this can be obtained is by use of the pressure canner. Be sure to review what we have said in Chapter 2 on canning if need be.

Since we have noted previously that fat in canned meat can cause the rubber sealing rings to deteriorate, we should note that certain cuts of pork contain a great amount of fat; therefore these cuts are better off cured than canned. Such examples would be hams, and shoulders. Cuts of pork that are most frequently canned are lean trimmings in sausage, loins, meat from spareribs, hearts and tongues.

Pages 88 through 95 in Chapter 6 on beef contain instructions for canning meat. These instructions pertain to pork as well as to beef, veal, lamb, mutton, and large game animals. For that reason they are not repeated here, and you are advised to refer to these pages for instructions for canning your pork. Suffice it to say here that the yield of five to five and a half pounds of fresh untrimmed loin will about fill a one-quart jar.

Freezing

You are referred to Chapter 3 on freezing for guidance in the freezing of pork.

The USDA recommends that pork be frozen within five days after slaughter because additional chilling for purposes of aging does not improve it. It should be used within six or eight months.

We know that salt causes meat to become rancid quickly, especially when meat is frozen, and since sausage and cured meats contain quantities of salt, these should be used within two to four months after being frozen. Cured meats should best not be frozen unless they are first cooked, for they lose much of their goodness if frozen first. But if you have cuts you plan to cure, freeze them first if you cannot cure them right away; then cure them after they have thawed.

Curing

Chapter 4 covers the fundamentals on curing, and it might be well to review it before proceeding further.

Since Farmers' Bulletin No. 2138 covers the subject of curing pork in considerable detail, we shall quote it pretty much as is for this section of the chapter.

"Pork is cured in three ways - with salt alone, with salt and sugar, or with salt, sugar, and saltpeter. The last is the preferred 'sugar cure.' You can sugar-cure pork either dry or in sweet-pickle brine. Because the dry cure is usually faster when curing meat on the farm, it is popular in the South where warm weather makes spoilage a serious problem.

"With either the dry or sweet-pickle cure remember the main essentials:

Chill the meat and keep it cold.

Use the amount of salt in the recipe.

Give the meat enough curing time to absorb the salt thoroughly.

Smoke cured meat long enough to drive out excess moisture.

"Weigh meat and curing ingredients carefully. Too little salt may cause spoilage; too much salt makes hard, dry, oversalty meat.

"Keep meat cold while in the cure. Hold curing meat at a temperature near 36°F to 40°F. Higher temperatures increase the chance of spoilage. Lower temperatures slow salt penetration.

"If curing temperatures drop below freezing for several days, add the same number of days to curing time. Temperatures below 36°F slow salt penetration.

"Frozen meat is difficult to handle. If fresh meat freezes, thaw it in a chill room or in cold brine before putting it in cure.

"Figure curing time carefully. Too few days in cure may cause spoilage. Too long in a cure in heavy salt results in loss of quality.

Dry Curing

"Check internal temperature of heaviest hams. Be sure it is below 40°F.

"Weigh the trimmed meat and the right amount of curing material. For 100 pounds* of ham or shoulder use:

Salt - 8 pounds

Sugar - 2 pounds (brown, white, or syrup)

Saltpeter - 2 ounces

*Author's Note: For lesser amounts of meat, cut amounts of ingredients proportionately.

For bacon and other thin cuts, use only one-half this amount.

"Mix ingredients thoroughly, be especially careful to mix the finely powdered saltpeter through the salt.

"Divide the curing mixture into two about equal parts, one part to use at once, the other to save for resalting. For bacon and other thin cuts, use the required amount at once; do not resalt.

"Rub one part of curing mixture on all surfaces of meat, poking some into shank ends. Pat about a 1/8-inch layer on lean face of hams. Pat a thin covering on shoulder. 'Frost' the thin bacon strip with the mixture - the heavier the cut, the greater its share of the mixture.

"Fit salted meat in a clean barrel or crock, being careful not to shake off the curing mixture. Hold in a cold place, 36°F to 40°F.

"Figure time in cure (a minimum of 25 days): Bacon - 1½ days to the pound; hams and shoulders - 2 days to the pound. Check curing time on calendar.

"Resalt with other half of curing mixture 6 to 8 days after meat is put in cure. Salt hams and shoulders as before. For bacon and other thin cuts, add no more curing mixture. Keep pack cold, 36°F to 40°F.

"Give the salt plenty of time to penetrate to the center of the cuts and distribute itself evenly through the piece (2 or 3 days to the pound, per piece, dry cure).

"All the surface salt may be absorbed into the dry-cured meat before curing time is up. Give it more time to work down into the center of the cuts.

"On the farm, meat often has to be cured at temperatures above 40°F. Under these conditions, speed up salt penetration.

Salt lightly and spread the fresh warm cuts.

(Never pile warm meat or blanket it with salt.)

Poke salt into the joints.

Bone or slice the cuts into smaller, more quickly salted pieces.

"All these methods help and may save the meat, but none are so satisfactory as curing at the proper temperature - 36°F to 40°F."

USDA Bulletin 2138 also points out that six pounds of salt per 100 pounds of trimmed pork is adequate for a more palatable salt taste and will cure the pork properly providing all the mixture is carefully packed into the shanks and patted on the faces of the hams and shoulders.

Brine, or Sweet Pickle Curing

Here is what Bulletin 2138 says about sweet pickle curing:

"Fit the cold, smoothly trimmed cuts into a clean barrel or crock. Cover with a cold pickle solution (36°F to 40°F)* made by dissolving 8 pounds of salt, 2 pounds of sugar, and 2 ounces of saltpeter in 4½ gallons of water. Weight the meat to keep it from floating above the pickle solution. Use enough pickle solution to submerge the meat. Keep pack cold throughout curing period - at 36°F to 40°F if possible.

"Overhaul the pack about the seventh day after putting it in cure by removing all the meat, pouring out the sweet pickle, repacking the meat, and covering with the restirred curing mixture. Overhaul two more times - about the 14th and 28th days.

"Curing time for hams and shoulders is 3½ to 4 days to the pound, with a minimum of 28 days for the light-weight cuts. Thus, a 6-pound shoulder needs 28 days in the cure; a 15-pound ham, 60 days. However, a 10-pound bacon needs 15 days in cure; heavier bacon and loins, 21 days.

"Bacon may receive a milder cure if you use 5½ instead of 4½ gallons of water to make the sweet pickle.

"Pickled pork may be left in curing solution until used, but it is rather salty.

"If the sweet-pickle solution sours or becomes ropy or sirupy, discard it. Scrub the meat in hot water, scald and rechill the barrel, repack the meat, and cover with new, cold, curing solution. Use 5½ gallons of water to make this second solution instead of 4½ recommended above."

---

*Author's Note: Below 38°F is best. USDA says that brine has a tendency to become stringy when temperature is above 38°F.

Because the bones in a ham are ideal places for harmful bacteria to lodge and start spoilage, one is well advised to bone out the ham before curing. Once the ham is boned, rub the curing mixture well into the area where the bone was located. Boning the ham before curing has saved many a person from ending up with a spoiled cure. If you pump hams, boning is not necessary.

Once the cure time is up, the pieces should be removed from the dry or brine mixture and hung to dry after first soaking them for fifteen to thirty minutes in cold water to remove surface salt. Meat should be strung for hanging by passing string through the shank of hams and shoulders; a skewer of wood or galvanized wire through a slab of bacon will provide adequate support for hanging it. All meat should then be scrubbed with a firm brush and water of about 110-125°F; this action will give the meat a lighter color when smoked. Hang meat to dry until you are ready to smoke it; and at least overnight to prevent if from streaking when being smoked. If you do not wish to smoke it, let it hang for a week; then bag it for safe keeping.

Smoking

Chapter 5 describes the fundamentals of building a smokehouse.

Once the hams, shoulders, bacon, and other pieces to be smoked are hung in the smoke chamber, a fire should be built and raised to the temperature of about 100°F-120°F the first day. This action, with the vents wide open, will drive out moisture. Next day close the vents and allow the meat to smoke over a cold smoke (90°F) for one or more days - the length of time depending on the amount of smoke flavor you wish and the desired color you wish to obtain on the finished pieces. A stiff wire run into the very middle of the meat pieces and withdrawn will carry the internal odor to you, and you can tell if it is to your liking. If, however, the odor is unpleasant, the piece should be cut open and examined for possible spoilage.

Assuming everything is fine, the meat should be bagged as described earlier on page 65.

You will always find someone who has had great luck storing smoked meat for long periods of time without bagging and without any spoilage. Don't let these experiences become the ground rules for you to follow. You might be successful; yet you are running a great risk that skipper flies and fly eggs will enter the meat and cause spoilage. Wrap and bag it properly and be safe. Properly wrapped and bagged, hams should keep many months - certainly well over a year. But bacon does not keep so well, and should be consumed within the next couple of seasons. Keep stored meat in a cool, dry place although such meat will store well in a refrigerator; and skipper flies will not multiply below 45°F although you may notice surface mold.

Surface mold does no harm, and it may be scraped or trimmed off. Applications of vegetable oil or lard will retard mold growth.

Expect smoked meat to lose up to one-quarter of its weight as fresh meat after it has been cured and smoked and stored for a year.

Smithfield Hams

The famous flavor of Smithfield-style hams is pungent and unique. It may be obtained by storing the smoked meat in heated storage of 105°F to 110°F for 50 to 70 days. Normal storage at room temperature over periods of nine months to a year will usually impart this Smithfield, or aged, flavor, too. Use the dry cure if you are planning to make a Smithfield ham.

What to Do With Fat

Pork Fat

Since this is a book of food processing, we'll concern ourselves with the food uses of pork fat; however it is worth noting that it, like other animal fats, can be used for soap and candle-making. There are some excellent books on these subjects on the market.* But for food uses of pork fat two

---

*"Making Homemade Soaps and Candles" by Phyllis Hobson, Garden Way Publishing Co., is a recent and recommended book covering these subjects.

things may be done: salting it down into what is commonly called "salt pork" and rendering it into lard.

Backfat is used for salt pork. After it is trimmed, it should be cured with dry salt, the pieces of backfat being packed in a container with holes in the bottom to allow moisture to drain out. Pack this just as you would any meat you pack for dry curing. Keep it well packed, from time to time inspecting to be sure. When fat is removed from the container for use, be certain the pieces remaining are well covered with salt. Fat kept this way will be useable for up to fifteen months.

Some prefer to pack backfat in large crocks instead of in containers that have holes in the bottom. This of course allows fluids extracted from the fat and from the air to build up and a brine will develop over a period of time. Even so, some have been fortunate in not having the fat spoil for quite some periods of time. We must say that they were lucky, but they were not playing safe. The safe way is to use the method described above. Should you wish to experiment with the latter, you would be well advised to overhaul the fat from time to time, scrubbing it, and repacking with new salt.

Leaf fat, backfat, and fat trimmings make excellent lard. While some use the caul and ruffle fat as well, this makes a darker colored lard; so it is best to use it separately rather than to mix it with the other types of fat. Rendering means cooking it until all the fat has melted and only the residual tissues, called "cracklings," remain. As the moisture is driven out of the fat, the temperature will rise; so take care not to let it spatter and burn yourself. Once the cracklings have turned brown and begun to settle, let the rendered lard cool, after which ladle it off into pails or other containers that will seal tightly for storage. The cracklings* may be pressed for further removal of lard. Store in a cool, dry, and dark place.

---

*After the cracklings have been pressed, you will have some great eating if you will put a little salt on them and mix them up with fried potatoes! Or break the pressed pieces up after they are cooled, and you will have some great munching bits for TV watching or for cocktail parties.

SAUSAGE

One of the things the homeowner usually looks forward to when he has meat for processing is making sausage. It is not true that sausage has to be pork although quite frankly pork is most frequently the most common meat ingredient. But sausage is best described as being ground meat: pork, beef, mutton, game, and even poultry or a combination of these meats that is usually highly seasoned with herbs, spices, and salt; and sometimes with the addition of cereals, animal blood, and almost endless other ingredients. The main ingredient, however, is ground meat. It is difficult to find a person who has not heard of frankfurters or farm sausage, bratwurst, liverwurst, bologna, salami. They are all different forms of sausage.

There is some debate as to whether sausage should be called a cured meat product or not. Some say yes and some say no; and it probably doesn't really matter. But those who say yes think of it as being cured because of the salt content and seasonings which they feel do indeed give it a "cured" effect. And some sausage recipes actually call for meat that has first been cured in the traditional manner.

The various meat trimmings should be saved for sausage making, and to those you may wish to add other meat cuts as suggested on pages 86, 103-104. Or use just any special meat cut you may prefer, even a ham, a shoulder, or bacon cut; the sausage won't mind, and you may find that the better the cut of meat the more delicate the flavor of your sausage. But, be certain all body areas and clots are cut away, or your sausage may spoil.

Just be sure, too, that you have a proportion of lean meat to fat that suits your taste. A general rule is one-third fat and two-thirds lean. More fat will cause the sausage to shrink considerably when cooked, and more lean is apt to make the sausage considerably more hard and dry than you may like. But you be the judge - work it out for yourself. A good way is to make a small sample before you make the main recipe and discover for yourself if you are satisfied with the amount of fat and lean. You will also have an opportunity to check the balance of the other ingredients to your own liking.

Some recipes may call for sausage to be smoked or to be air dried. But remember that sausage should always be cooked before it is eaten - either during the sausage-making process or prior to its being served.

A good meat grinder is a necessity when making sausage. And you will find it best to have a few grinding plates of different sizes; the ½-inch and the 1/8-inch are probably the ones most frequently used; but if you wish your sausage to be more finely or more coarsely ground, there are finer and coarser plates that will fit your grinder. (See Figures 7-2 and 7-3.)

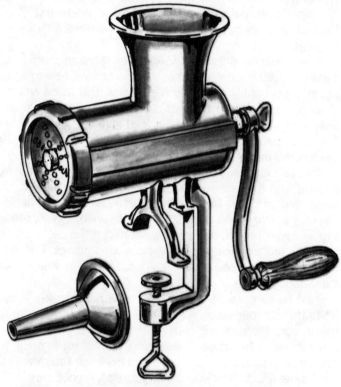

Hand-operated sausage grinder with funnel
for filling sausage casings.
Figure 7-2

An Electric Sausage Grinder
Figure 7-3

Chilled meat grinds up better than warm. Warm meat will give you a mushy result; so be sure it is well chilled and firm. Then add your herbs and other seasonings, mix well, and run everything through the coarse plate. You will notice that this grinding has warmed the meat somewhat; so set it aside in the refrigerator overnight to re-chill. This will also give the herbs and seasonings an opportunity to penetrate the meat. In the morning grind it again, but this time with the small plate. Should it be impossible to chill the meat enough to facilitate grinding, you may grind pieces of ice along with the meat to keep it cool.

Once the sausage is made, it may be stored in several different ways. Fresh sausage is frequently partially cooked; then packed in sterilized crocks and covered with melted lard until ready for use (see page 98 re. preserving with lard); then it is finally cooked before being served. It may be canned (see page 93) and it may be frozen or refrigerated. Some recipes for sausage call for it to be packed in muslin sleeves or in casings and then sometimes to be air dried, or air dried and smoked.

Casings are the intestines of sheep, cattle, and hogs. Beef casings may be used although they are apt to be rather tough; sheep or hog casings are best. And you should be able to order a bundle of casings, if need be, through your local butcher or from a local slaughterhouse. Argentina and Russia ship animal casings to the United States in considerable quantities for sausage makers.

Artificial casings are also available and are quite commonly used, especially in commercial packing houses. The skinless frankfurter is stuffed in artificial casings that may be removed once the frankfurter is made. Your local butcher may be able to obtain artificial casings if you prefer them, or contact a local slaughterhouse.

The Morton Salt Company has good instructions for preparing hog casings when the hog is being butchered, and the technique seems to be good for casings of other animals:

"If the intestines are to be run, this should be done while they are still warm. The start should be made where they leave the stomach. If the intestines are to be used for casings, the end should be tied and the thumb and forefinger of the left hand placed along the 'ruffle fat.' With the right hand the intestines are torn from the attached fat.

"Only the small intestines are generally used for casings, so when the large intestine is reached the fat is removed, the small intestine tied off, and the large intestine discarded.

"If the casings are to be used, the contents should be carefully stripped out and the casings thoroughly washed. Then reverse them by turning up a fold at the end of the casings like the cuff of a pair of trousers, and pour warm water into this fold. It is best to have one person hold the intestines, one to pour the water, and a third to 'feed' in the intestines as the weight of the water reverses them. To make the job easier cut the intestines into several lengths. The mucous coat, which is now on the outside after the intestines are reversed, can be scraped off with the back of the knife blade, or scraped through a sharpened notched stick by drawing the casing between the notch and the thumb. To do a good job of cleaning this operation should be repeated several times, and the casings washed in lukewarm water. If the casings are not to be used at once, they should be packed in dry salt until they are to be used."

When filling animal and artificial casings, you will want to tie them at the far end with a soft, but strong, string. They are best filled by using a stuffer which can be attached to your grinder. At regular intervals of several inches they should be tied again so a new sausage will be formed.

On the farm muslin sleeves are commonly used for stuffing sausages. These sleeves are 2½ to 3 inches in diameter and are sewn from regular muslin cloth by the housewife, then washed and dipped in paraffin before being filled with sausage.

When filling the casings and the muslin sleeves, be sure that every bit of space is filled with sausage. If air space remains anywhere, it is an open invitation for mold and for spoilage.

Muslin sleeves are packed by hand by stuffing them in lengths up to a foot-and-a-half to two feet. When slicing the sausage, one usually slices right through the muslin cloth, which is easily removed without disfiguring the sliced sausage.

Chapter 12 contains a variety of sausage recipes; you will find many others in standard cookbooks. But let's look now at the USDA's suggestion* for fresh farm sausage, which may be eaten fresh, canned, or stuffed in muslin sleeves or casings and refrigerated, or frozen.

First here is its little recipe for taste testing:

4 pounds trimmings
5 teaspoons salt
4 teaspoons ground sage
4 teaspoons ground pepper
½ teaspoon ground cloves or
1 teaspoon ground nutmeg (if desired)
1 teaspoon sugar

---

*USDA Bulletin No. 2138

Assuming you found the taste sample appealing, here is the recipe for 100 pounds of trimmings; but remember you can adjust the ingredients proportionately if you have more or less than 100 pounds:

> *1¾ pounds salt*
> *2 to 4 ounces sage*
> *2 to 4 ounces ground black pepper*
> *½ to 1 ounce red pepper (if desired)*
> *½ to 1 ounce ground cloves, or*
> *1 ounce ground nutmeg (if desired)*
> *12 ounces sugar (if sausage is to be used quickly)*

Thoroughly mix the seasoning, spread it over the trimmings and grind the whole quantity through the fine plate. You may prefer to grind the unseasoned meat through a plate with 1/2-inch holes and then mix it with the spices and regrind through a plate with 1/8-inch holes.

If you are stuffing the sausage into casings, do it immediately after grinding. The sausage should be soft enough to pack tightly in the casings without adding cold water.

To make bulk sausage that will slice and fry without crumbling add a scant half cup of cold water with the hands until the meat becomes sticky and doughlike.

8
LAMB

Special Note

Those of us who are fond of lamb, be it roasts, chops, ribs, or stews, will find that processing lamb is similar in many ways to processing pork and as easy to do. Lamb may be thought of as a delicate meat because it has so little fat, but the older sheep become well fatted and provide the tasty mutton. It also may be mixed with pork and other meats for very delicious sausages.

There is a common opinion that lamb does not have to be aged, that chilling to remove all body temperatures is sufficient. That is all right, but we have been impressed by well experienced butchers and meat connoisseurs who insist that lamb is improved by aging for at least two weeks except when the meat is to be frozen.

In any event, lamb should be chilled completely before being processed, or even cut up; this will make it easier to handle, will prevent deterioration, and will make the meat more tender. The USDA recommends a temperature between 34°F and 36°F and advises to avoid freezing. This same temperature may be used for aging if you decide to do that.

THE PRIMARY CUTS OF LAMB

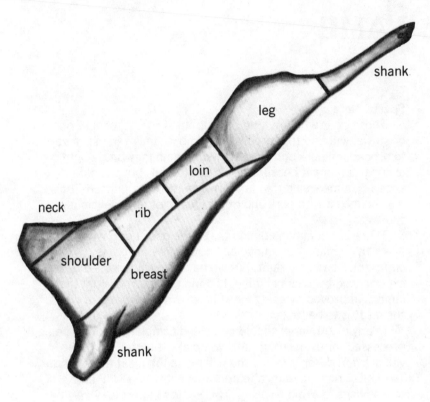

The Primary Cuts of Lamb
Figure 8-1

The Uses of the Primary Cuts of Lamb

The customary uses of these primary cuts are as follows:

Legs .... Roasts
Shoulders .... Roasts, chops, trimmings for stewing meat

Ribs	Chops and roasts
Loin...........................	Chops and roasts
Breasts	Roasts, stew or ground meat, spareribs
Neck..........................	Stew or ground meat
Shanks	Stew or ground meat

And like pork, there are three ways to process it: canning, freezing, and curing, followed if you like by smoking.

Yield

As much as 50% of the live weight of a lamb is lost during slaughter, cutting, and trimming. Approximately 75% of the carcass weight will be from legs, chops, and shoulders; 15% will be breast and other stew meat.

Canning

Follow the instructions of canning outlined in Chapter 2, remembering to trim off any excess fat since fat will cause the rubber seals on metal cans and jar lids to deteriorate as well as rubber rings. And to economize on space and to simplify the canning operation, bone out the cuts before canning and roll them.

Freezing

For details on freezing, review Chapter 3 and follow the instructions while freezing lamb.

Like other meats, the quality of lamb is not improved by freezing. It should be top quality to begin with.

It is recommmended that lamb be frozen within ten days following slaughter. Keeping it chilled in the interim at temperatures between 34°F and 36°F will make it easier to handle and to cut. If you remember to separate the chops with a double layer of wax paper, you will find them easier to separate when you are ready to thaw them. Remember, too, that if lamb is cooked before it is thawed, the time must be lengthened; ⅓ longer is the general rule for roasts and twice as long for chops.

The following * is the recommended storage time for lamb stored at 0°F after a fast freeze at -10°F.

Chops . . . . .3-4 months
Roasts . . . . .8-12 months
Ground . . . . .2-3 months
Stew . . . . .2-3 months

If lamb is kept frozen longer than a year, it is quite likely to be a disappointment.

Curing

Lamb is an excellent meat for curing. The ribs and loins take on superior cures; however they should first be split down the center of the backbone so the spinal cord may be removed, for it would otherwise spoil rapidly. And the legs and shoulders are especially good for smoking.
During the cure, maintain a temperature between 36°F and 38°F.
Either brine or dry curing may be used.

Dry Cure
For a dry cure, the following is recommended** for 100 pounds of lamb:

---

*USDA Farmers' Bulletin No. 2152
**Ibid

        5 pounds of salt
        4 pounds of sugar
        4 ounces of saltpeter

Use only two-thirds of the mixture for rubbing into the meat and for packing. Between the 3rd and 5th days of curing, the pack should be overhauled using the other third of the mixture. Meat may remain in the cure until it is used unless it is to be removed for smoking, in which case it should remain in the cure the same length of time as for brine cure.

Brine Cure

The following is recommended* for 100 pounds of lamb:

        8 pounds of salt
        2 pounds of white or brown sugar
        2 ounces of saltpeter
        6 gallons of cold water

Meat should be packed in accordance with instructions in Chapter 4. It should be overhauled between the 3rd and the 5th days of the cure, with the same brine.

Breasts, loins, and ribs should be ready in ten to fourteen days, legs and shoulders in 25 to 40 days, although small legs will likely be ready in 25 to 30 days. Watch that the brine does not become ropy; if it does, follow instructions in Chapter 4 for remedying the situation.

Smoking

When cuts for smoking have been selected, they should be scrubbed with a stiff brush and hot water to remove salt caked on the outside surface; then hung up to dry. Two days of smoking at temperatures of 100°F to 120°F will normally be

*USDA Farmers' Bulletin No. 2152

sufficient. (You will note that this temperature is slightly higher than what we used for smoking hams.)

If you smoke mutton, be on guard that a temperature as high as 120°F does not cause fat to drip, setting up flames in the fire pit that will be intense enough to start cooking the mutton.

Normal room temperature will keep well-wrapped smoked lamb for several months providing it is cooled thoroughly following smoking and wrapped tightly in muslin or paper. And be certain that the room is dry.

Since lamb tends to dry out quickly, you will want to use the thinner cuts first or else can it.

9
POULTRY

Special Note

Poultry is such a satisfactory meat, for it may be used in many ways, and it is highly nutritious.

When we think of poultry, we think not only of chicken but also of turkeys, geese, ducks, guinea hens, and squab; and the directions for processing chicken will apply to these other kinds of fowl also unless specifically mentioned or excepted from the discussion.

Because of the high water content in fowl, it should be cared for promptly; otherwise it will spoil very quickly.

Inspection and Grading

The United States Department of Agriculture provides federal inspection for wholesomeness of poultry that is sold in interstate commerce and overseas. Its stamp may assure the buyer that the bird is "from a healthy flock, is processed under rigid sanitary conditions, contains no harmful chemicals or

Federal Poultry Inspection Stamp
Figure 9-1

additives, is properly packaged and truthfully and informatively labeled.*

The USDA also grades such poultry; the top grade, representing the finest possible, is U.S. Grade A.

Federal Poultry Grading Stamp
Figure 9-2

Cutting Up Poultry

We shall assume that a chicken or other type of fowl has been slaughtered, drawn, rinsed in cold water, and wiped dry; and now we'll indicate steps** for cutting it up:

1 Disjoint the chicken. It helps to pull on the leg or wing while cutting through the joints.
2 Cut from the end of the breastbone to the backbone along the ribs. Separate the breast and the back. Break the backbone and cut the back in half.
3 Cut the breast straight down between the wishbone and the point of breast, leaving the meat on the wishbone.
4 Remove the breast meat from the center bone by carving down the bone on one side of the breast. Repeat this on the other side of the breastbone.

---

*USDA Home and Garden Bulletin No. 110
** Based on USDA Home and Garden Bulletin No. 106

5 Cut the legs into drumsticks and thighs. Saw the drumsticks off short, if desired. Sort into meaty and bony pieces, and set aside the giblets (heart, gizzard, neck, etc.) for separate use.

A good sharp knife and a pair of meat shears will simplify this job a great deal. If you have a large bird, such as a turkey, you will find it easy to cut the larger pieces into yet smaller pieces for convenience in canning and freezing.

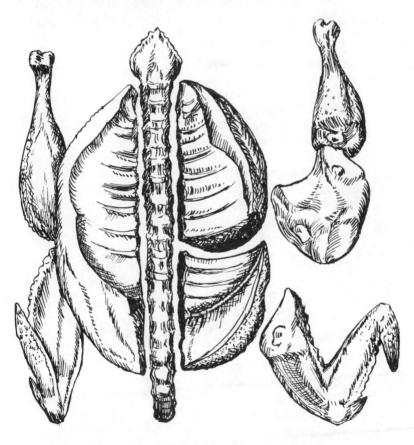

Poultry Cut Up for Canning or Freezing
Figure 9-3

Canning *

Preparation for canning is covered in Chapter 2.

Poultry may be canned by the hot pack or raw pack method; and it may be canned with bone in the meat or without bone.

It is simple to make broth if you are planning hot pack by putting the bony pieces in cold water, letting them simmer until the meat on the bones is tender and done, skimming off the fat, straining the broth if need be; and there you have it ready to fill the cans and jars once they have been filled with meat.

1 **Directions for cut-up poultry.**

Hot pack, with bone. Bone the breast. Saw drumsticks off short. Leave the bone in other meaty pieces. Trim off large lumps of fat because excess fat can cause the rubber seals of cans and jars to deteriorate.

Place the raw meaty pieces in a pan and cover with hot broth or water. Put on lid. Heat, stirring occasionally until meat is medium done. To test, cut a piece at the center; if the pink color is almost gone, the meat is medium done.

Pack poultry loosely. Place the thighs and drumsticks with skin next to glass or tin. Fit the breasts into the center and small pieces where needed.

1 In glass jars. Pack the jars, leaving one inch of space above poultry. Add salt if desired: ½ teaspoon per pint or 1 teaspoon per quart. Cover poultry with boiling broth, leaving one inch of headspace at top of jar. Adjust jar lids. Process at 10 pounds pressure (240°F).

Pint jars . . . . .65 minutes
Quart jars . . . . .75 minutes

*Based on USDA Home and Garden Bulletin No. 106

2 In tin cans. Pack the cans, leaving ½ inch of
   headspace above poultry. Add salt if desired: ½
   teaspoon to No. 2 cans or ¾ teaspoon to No. 2½
   cans. Fill cans to top with boiling broth. Seal.
   Process in a pressure canner at 10 pounds
   pressure (240°F).

   No. 2 cans .... 55 minutes
   No. 2½ cans .... 75 minutes

Hot pack without bone. Remove bone - but not the
skin - from meaty pieces either before or after
precooking.

1 In glass jars. Pack the jars loosely with hot
   poultry leaving one inch of headspace above
   poultry. Add salt if desired: ½ teaspoon per pint
   or 1 teaspoon per quart. Pour in boiling broth;
   leave 1 inch of space at top of jar. Adjust jar
   lids. Process in a pressure canner at 10 pounds
   pressure (240°F).

   Pint jars .... 75 minutes
   Quart jars .... 90 minutes

2 In tin cans. Pack loosely, leaving ½ inch above
   poultry. Add salt if desired: ½ teaspoon to No. 2
   cans, ¾ teaspoon to No. 2½ cans. Fill the cans to
   the top with boiling broth. Seal. Process in a
   pressure canner at 10 pounds pressure (240°F).

   No. 2 cans .... 65 minutes
   No. 2½ cans ...,,. .... 90 minutes

Raw pack with bone. Bone the breast. Saw
drumsticks off short. Leave the bone in other
meaty pieces. Trim off large lumps of fat.
   Pack the raw poultry loosely. Place the thighs
and drumsticks with skin next to the glass or tin.
Fit the breasts into the center and small pieces
where needed.

1 In glass jars. Pack the jars to within one inch of
   the top. To exhaust air, cook raw poultry in the

jars at a slow boil to 170°F, or until medium done (about 75 minutes). Add salt if desired: ½ teaspoon per pint or 1 teaspoon per quart. Adjust lids. Process in a pressure canner at 10 pounds pressure (240°F).

    Pint jars . . . . .65 minutes
    Quart jars .75 minutes

2 In tin cans. Pack cans to top. To exhaust air, cook raw poultry in cans at slow boil to 170°F or until medium done (about 50 minutes). Add salt if desired: ½ teaspoon to No. 2 cans or ¾ teaspoon to No. 2½ cans. Seal cans. Process in a pressure canner at 10 pounds pressure (240°F).

    No. 2 cans .55 minutes
    No. 2½ cans . . . . .75 minutes

Raw pack without bone. Remove bone, but not skin, from meaty pieces before packing in containers.

1 In glass jars. Pack raw poultry in jars to 1 inch of the top. To exhaust air, cook poultry in jars at slow boil to 170°F, or until medium done (about 75 minutes). Add salt if desired: ½ teaspoon per pint or 1 teaspoon per quart. Adjust lids. Process in a pressure canner at 10 pounds pressure (240°F).

    Pint jars . . . . .75 minutes
    Quart jars .90 minutes

2 In tin cans. Pack raw poultry to top of cans. To exhaust air, cook poultry in cans at slow boil to 170°F, or until medium done (about 50 minutes). Add salt if desired: ½ teaspoon to No. 2 cans or ¾ teaspoon to No. 2½ cans. Seal cans. Process in a pressure canner at 10 pounds pressure (240°F).

    No. 2 cans .65 minutes
    No. 2½ cans . . . . .90 minutes

2 **Directions for giblets.**

If you wish to can giblets, use the smaller jars or cans (pints or No. 2 size). Wash and drain and pack gizzards and hearts together, but pack the livers by themselves after cooking; otherwise their strong flavor will mask the flavor of the other giblets. Use hot pack for giblets. Precook until medium done in a covered pan with hot broth or hot water.

1 In glass jars. Leave 1 inch of space above giblets. Add boiling water or boiling broth, leaving 1 inch of headspace. Adjust lids. Process in a pressure canner at 10 pounds pressure (240°F).
Pint jars . . . . .75 minutes
2 In tin cans. Leave ½ inch of space above giblets. Fill cans to top with boiling broth or boiling water. Seal. Process in a pressure canner at 10 pounds pressure (240°F).
No. 2 cans . . . . .65 minutes

Yield
For a one-quart jar of ready-to-cook chicken, untrimmed with bone in, you may expect to use the following amount when canning:
Canned with bone . . . . .3½ to 4¼ pounds
Canned without bone . . . . .5½ to 6¼ pounds

Freezing

It would be well to review Chapter 3 on freezing before proceeding to freeze poultry.
Following are some special notations to be considered when freezing fowl:

- **Freshly killed fowl are best for freezing.** If birds are young, consider them for roasts, for frying, and for broiling; older birds are best for stews and for braising.
- **Uncooked fowl should be cut up similarly** to the description given above for cutting up before canning. However, fowl may also be frozen whole.
- **If fowl are purchased in a store,** they should be unwrapped and re-wrapped before freezing.
- **Chill the fowl** in your refrigerator for twelve hours before freezing to insure its maximum tenderness.
- **Wrap and freeze** giblets separately, or they may be packaged separately and wrapped inside the bird providing you plan to use the bird within three months, which is about the maximum time giblets should be stored frozen.
- **Fowl should not be stuffed before freezing.** This would invite spoilage because of the slow temperature changes in the stuffing when fowl is frozen and later thawed.
- **Fowl is best thawed in the refrigerator** with the wrapping left intact; however it may also be thawed in cold water providing it is in a water-tight bag or wrapper. It will take up to two or three days to thaw a whole chicken weighing 4 or more pounds, while a 2-5 pound duck will require about 1½ days and a large goose will require a couple of days. Whole turkeys over 18 pounds 2-3 days; those with less weight 1-2 days.
- **It is frequently an advantage to have a large fowl cut in halves** before freezing if the whole bird is not likely to be required for the table all at one time.
- **If cooked meat is frozen, you would be well advised to pack it solidly** and then cover it with broth or gravy after first removing any bone. The addition of gravy or broth further eliminates air around the meat and is a precaution against an off-flavor that sometimes occurs. It also adds to the storage time of frozen cooked fowl.

- **When wrapping whole birds, be sure the legs and wings are wrapped tight against the body;** it might help to tie them first. Wrap tightly to drive out all the excess air possible.
- **What are the best birds for freezing whole?** Chickens, ducks, geese, and turkeys rate high.

Flash-freeze poultry at -10°F and store at 0°F. The maximum recommended storage time* for home-frozen poultry is as follows:

	Months
Uncooked poultry:	
Chicken and turkey	12
Duck and goose	6
Giblets	3
Cooked poultry:	
Slices or pieces -	
Covered with broth or gravy	6
Not covered with broth or gravy	1
Sandwiches of poultry meat	1
Cooked poultry dishes	6
Fried chicken	4

Curing and Smoking

Although curing and smoking fowl is not so common as with other types of meat, there is no reason to believe it cannot be done successfully and with pleasant results. However, anything under three and a half pounds dressed weight will probably be less satisfactory than heavier birds. Chickens, capons, ducks, and turkeys (yes, especially turkeys) are best; the fatter the

*USDA Home and Garden Bulletin No. 70

better, and attention should be paid to see that they are top quality and with perfect skin condition.

Whether you use a dry cure or a brine cure is strictly up to you; but in either instance when the bird is drawn, the feet, lower legs (shank), and head must be cut off. Some even remove the neck.

Curing fowl is simple and the procedure is the same as outlined in Chapter 4. The curing mixture or brine is similar to that used for hams, and it is quite likely that you may wish to add some of your own special spices.

Close attention must be given to assure that the bird is completely cleaned with no blood or waste particles in evidence. If you can also pull out the leg tendons without damaging the skin in the drumsticks, do so, for this will enable the cure to penetrate the leg muscles better.

Birds should stay in the dry cure or brine at approximately 34°F - 36°F for the entire cure in order for the salt to have maximum effect. Time in the cure is probably best related to the weight of the bird; and from a day and a half to two days per pound of dressed bird is about right. If dry cure is used, be sure to get the salt mixture rubbed well inside the body cavity.

In the event you may wish to pump the bird with brine solution, insert the needle (best to use a small size needle) with the same solution as you will use to cover the bird, once in each leg, once in each thigh, once in each wing, a couple times in the back, and five or six times in the breast. Ten percent of the bird's weight is sufficient brine to pump into the bird.

Even though the birds may not be in the cure for a long period of time, check the container occasionally to determine if everything is in proper order and the birds are well submerged in the brine.

Once the bird has been removed from the curing process, it should be washed thoroughly to remove all salt; inspect it well to be certain that no salt remains in the body cavity. Soaking it first in fresh, cold water for an hour or more will help remove most of the salt. Then it should be hung for about ten or twelve hours to dry thoroughly. If you did not remove the neck, you may hang it up by the neck; or you may wish to put it in a stockinette so it will drain; if the latter, hang it legs up.

Another simple way to hang the bird is to encircle the body with smooth twine under the wing section and hang it; this should allow it to drain and dry thoroughly.

When you are certain the bird is well drained and dried, it is ready for the smokehouse. It should be hung there in a manner similar to when drying - neck up, or breast down and legs up if in stockinette.

Smoke to achieve the desired color rather than trying to determine smoking time with a watch; endeavor to obtain a rich golden brown or a dark mahogany color according to your wishes. And be sure your fire provides cold smoke so as not to cook the bird; 90°F would be hot enough.

Of course the longer a bird is smoked, the more weight it will lose, but even so you would do well to stay away from smoke hotter than 90°F.

When smoking is done, wrap and store your bird according to previous instructions.

Since turkeys are frequently rather large birds to handle easily, you may wish to have yours sawed in two, straight down through the breast and backbone from head to tail. This should not present any problems in connection with curing and smoking.

A goose is less satisfactory to smoke unless you smoke just the breast and legs. After curing and washing, these parts are best dried and smoked in stockinette. You will still find some lean meat on the wings, the neck, and the back; this may be scraped off after the cure and wrapped and tied in skin from the neck for smoking, or it may be packed into sausage casings and smoked.

10
GAME

Some Like It Wild

Throughout the early days of our country, game sustained the pioneers during many a long and perilous winter. Most parts of our country flourished with game at that time; and had it not been for its availability, starvation would have taken the lives of countless more of the early settlers. Town histories and the diaries of these pioneers are full of references to the many kinds and great quantities of wild animals and birds that inhabited our land in those early times.

Over the years we have seen a tendency in the United States to depend less and less on the wild for food; instead our diets have constantly been supplied with greater amounts of beef and veal, pork, lamb, and domesticated fowl.

As a result, many persons have never even tasted wild meat; and many seem reluctant to try, their main reason frequently being that wild meat is reported to have an unpleasant, "too gamey" taste.*

The experienced hunters and woodsmen understand this "gamey" complaint; yet they also know that, properly prepared, game can achieve heights in succulence and delight that is seldom equalled elsewhere. But they know, too, the "gamey" complaint can be real if one does not know what to do to prevent it.

---

*Do not confuse the unpleasant gamey taste with the "wild" taste that is so sought after.

Prevention is simple, but short-cuts must be ruled out; for unless one takes care to be thorough and diligent, his reward will not be good eating.

Succulent and tasteful wild meat depends on:

1 Immediate field dressing of the kill.
2 Immediate chilling and continued chilling until the animal or bird is processed or eaten.
3 Proper cooking. This may require removal of much of the animal fat if it seems to be the source of the "gamey" odor and substituting beef suet or pork fat when cooking.

There is, however, some evidence that more and more game is being taken by hunters each year not only as a by-product of the sport but also as a way to hold down the food budget. State Fish and Game Departments are controlling the wild herds and flocks in an attempt to make them more plentiful for the hunter, and in certain areas of the states new game is being re-introduced into habitats that were common for it years and years ago.

Annually we see many thousands of deer, elk, and other large game animals being transported atop automobiles during season by local and out-of-state hunters. States also have open seasons for ducks, turkeys, antelope, moose, and for most of the other animals and birds as well. It has been estimated that over 45,000,000 wild rabbits are shot each year by lucky hunters, over 14,000,000 wild ducks, 8,000,000 pheasants, 22,000,000 quail, a million wild geese, and at least 470,000 wild turkeys.

To regulate the wild herds, state and federal governments frequently find it necessary to thin them down to prevent weakening of offspring through in-breeding and lack of adequate forage. And sometimes such animals are available for the public to purchase for home consumption. Should one wish a buffalo for his freezer, for instance, he would do well to contact one of the western state parks, or contact Buffalo Marketing Associates, Box 882, Rapid City, South Dakota 57701, to determine if and when buffalo are available, at what price, and how shipment would be made to one's home city. Queries for other animals may be similarly made.

Wild game will continue to be plentiful so long as it is not wasted and so long as state and federal laws governing the taking of wild game are observed. There is no excuse for a hunter's wasting game; and the experienced hunter knows that in order not to waste it, game must be immediately field dressed, chilled, and properly prepared for consumption. Short-cuts only result in waste and spoilage. He knows, too, that most states have regulations pertaining to the number and kind of game and fowl that may be taken and the maximum length of time such may be stored at home to be within these regulations; such information is readily available from the Fish and Wildlife Departments of every state or from the state Conservation Department.

While we are not attempting to be a cookbook (there are so many very excellent ones available) or a guide to field care of the kill, some understanding of the latter is perhaps desirable here since it is so basic in preventing the "gamey" taste from invading meat.

FIELD DRESSING *

A number of booklets and articles have been written on how to field dress game. Some of these disagree on how the game should be positioned or on some other detail of no great importance; but they all agree that all wild game should be bled completely, have its entrails removed, and be chilled,

---

*Source information for field dressing game may be found in a number of books and pamphlets including the following:

"Good Eating From the Woods," pamphlet published by Michigan State University Extension Service in cooperation with the Michigan Department of Conservation, East Lansing, Michigan.

"Dressing Out Your Deer," pamphlet published by The Penn State University, College of Agriculture Extension Service, University Park, Pennsylvania, Special Circular 119.

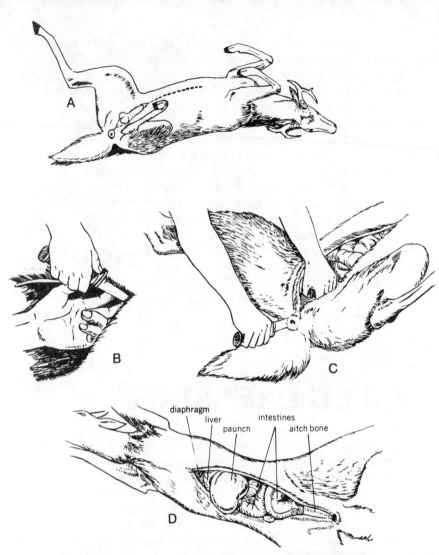

Field dressing a deer: (A) With rump slightly lower than shoulder, deer is positioned on its back with hind legs spread. Make a cut through hide and muscle along centerline from base of tail to breastbone as noted. (B) Guide knife with free hand to prevent puncture of paunch and intestines. (C) Make cut around anus to free and draw it away from carcass when intestines and stomach are

Figure 10-1

140 *Game*

immediately following the kill. To do otherwise can only invite spoilage since harmful bacteria will start to spread at once. As soon as the entrails are removed, the body cavity should be wiped clean with grass, paper, or cloth but should not be washed out, sponged, or wiped with wet material, for this will cause bacteria to spread. The body cavity, which will have been split open to remove the entrails, should be kept open by the use of props (such as sticks) so the carcass may chill and all the body temperature be removed. And the carcass should be transported from the field to home in open air to keep it chilled. Once home, chilling should be continued at just about 32°F for times stated for other similar animals such as beef and domestic fowl.

There is some debate as to whether or not small game animals should be skinned in the field immediately following their slaughter; one of the considerations concerns whether or not the skin has value as fur.

Fowl, likewise, must be field dressed, this requiring that their entrails be removed, that the body cavity be wiped clean, and that the body temperature be removed by chilling.

Again in this book we must warn that if there is any doubt whatsoever that your game is not healthy and sound, be certain to have it inspected by a veterinarian before it is eaten or processed. Bear are very susceptible to trichinosis (see page 101 for instructions for killing the trichinae worms), and rabbits frequently have tularemia. Rabbits should be handled with rubber gloves while being field dressed to be certain that any tularemia bacteria are not transmitted to the hunter; and, during field dressing, the liver should be inspected for small white spots. If these are not found, and if the liver otherwise appears sound and healthy, the rabbit may be assumed to be healthy. Hunters should carry some disinfectant to scrub their hands with in the event any tularemia bacteria are present.

---

rolled out. Do not cut or break bladder. (D) Pull out lungs and heart after first cutting around diaphragm and cutting windpipe and gullet loose. Roll deer with body face down to drain all blood from body cavity. Save heart and liver if desired.

Large Game Animals

The careful hunter will endeavor to shoot his quarry in the neck, lung area, or in the heart; and he will field dress it immediately. Many of the large game animals have very little fat, the deer being one. They should not have their hides removed while aging if such be the case; otherwise they will dry out quickly and the meat will be tasteless. Ideally the temperature should be held to 32°-36°F during the aging process. Young animals should be aged for a week or so while older ones may be aged for two to three weeks. Aging is necessary inasmuch as the meat would have little or no flavor without it.

When cutting up large game, treat it similarly to beef. The tougher cuts should be made into ground meat or sausage, it having pork fat or suet added. And when cooked, meat having little or no fat should have strips of bacon or other fat cooked with it. A good idea is to slit the meat in a number of places with a knife and interlard strips of bacon or fat to cook along with the wild cut.

Canning
Review Chapter 2 on Canning and follow the same instructions you would if canning beef.

Freezing
Review Chapter 3 on Freezing and proceed as if you were freezing beef.

Curing and Smoking
Although it is not so common to cure and smoke big game, there really is no reason why it may not be done. Certainly the early pioneers used salt to preserve wild meat and with great success. If you wish to cure and smoke your deer, antelope, elk, moose, or other wild game, go right ahead just as if you were curing and smoking beef. You will find these animals are excellent for corning, too, and you may also wish to consider making some pemmican or jerky (see Chapter 12 for recipes).

Small Game Animals

Frequently small game animals will be skinned in the field when the animal is field dressed. This makes it much easier for the animal temperature to be chilled out more quickly than would happen otherwise, and the skin is removed more easily before the carcass has chilled.

Many small animals have scent glands which must be removed to prevent the meat from being overpowered in odor and flavor with a strong animal scent. These glands vary in

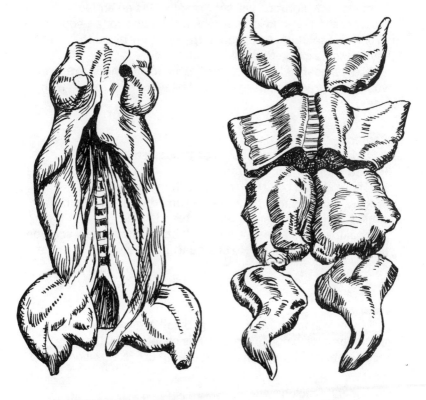

Rabbits and similar small game animals are easily cut up for processing.

Figure 10-2

color from a light yellow in the muskrat to a reddish and waxy color in the rabbit. Sometimes they appear as fatty globules and sometimes as small pea-like glands, depending on the type of animal. They may be found along the small of the back, along the spine area, and under the front legs. All traces of them must be removed; then the carcass should be chilled for one day anyway, and preferably for a couple days. Anytime the carcass is transported, it should be done in the open and not in a box or in the trunk of a car where cool air cannot circulate.

It is especially important when field dressing small game animals to examine all areas where the gunshot penetrated the body, for unless this area is especially well examined to remove all blood, deterioration will set in rapidly. As an added assurance it is a good idea to soak the carcass for an hour in a strong salt solution; salt should draw out any blood that may have become clogged in the wound.

Many a gourmet prefers small game to all others. Squirrel, woodchuck, raccoon, muskrat, and beaver are favorites with many.

Canning

Small game animals should be processed like chicken. Review Chapter 2 on Canning.

There should be little trouble cutting them up for processing. They may be disjointed and divided in a manner similar to the way chicken was prepared.

Soaking small game for an hour before canning in a solution of one tablespoon of salt to one quart of water often improves it.

Freezing

Review Chapter 3 on Freezing. Small game present no special problems not covered in this chapter. Maximum recommended storage time in freezer at 0°F is 4 - 6 months.

Curing and Smoking

Small game is not so frequently cured and smoked as large game. Presumably this is because it is consumed for its flavor so soon after killing, and little is left over for curing. But there are no reasons why one should not cure small game and even smoke it if one desires. It is not necessary to cut up rabbits and similar-size animals if one prefers to cure them whole.

Fowl

Game birds, too, must have their entrails removed as soon as shot, and their body cavity should be spread open to allow air to move through it and to remove body temperature and keep the carcass cool. The body cavity should be wiped dry as soon as eviscerated, for allowing moisture to remain within would invite the spread of harmful bacteria. Special care should be taken not to break the gall bladder sac when removing the entrails, because bile will ruin the meat flavor.

Most hunters prefer to hang their birds for three or four days at least and often up to ten; this should be done with the plumage still on; such aging in a temperature of about 40°F will tenderize the bird, improve its flavor, and make it easier to cut up for processing. When removing the plumage, be sure to pluck rather than skin the bird, the skin left intact will prevent moisture escaping from the meat when being cooked, and the flavor will be improved.

Some prefer rather than plucking off the feathers to dip the bird in a cool solution of two melted cakes of paraffin and a gallon of water that has been brought to a boil. The feathers will harden as the bird is withdrawn from a quick dip in the solution, and the feathers and wax may be scraped off together.

The oil sac from the base of the tail should also be removed before cooking or processing.

Canning
Review Chapter 2 on Canning and treat as you would chicken.

Freezing
Review Chapter 3 on Freezing and treat as you would chicken.

The maximum recommended time for storage in a freezer at 0°F is 4 - 6 months; ducks and geese will store satisfactorily for from 9 - 10 months as a rule.

Curing and Smoking

Wild birds may be cured and smoked similarly to domesticated fowl. See pages 133-135.

11
FISH

Food For Thought...

Fish is a very versatile kind of food. It comes from fresh water and from salt water. We have fin fish as well as shellfish. And fish, depending on the kind, may be canned, frozen, cured, and smoked. It is sometimes dried in the open air and sometimes pickled. It is much sought after and is high in nutritive value.

But fish is extremely fragile in terms of storage; it spoils in short order if not consumed quickly, or processed quickly for later use. Freshly caught fish has been known to spoil in the boat, or in the fisherman's basket even before he could get home. It is most important, then, that it be kept cool as soon as caught and maintained cool right up to the time it is cooked or processed; that is why the careful fisherman will provide a means to pack his catch in ice as soon as it is caught. And he knows, too, that it must be eviscerated and bled thoroughly as soon as caught.

Does it pay to process fish? Probably not, unless it is fish you have caught yourself or did not have to purchase. Except for the convenience, you would probably save money by purchasing either fresh fish or fish already processed. But keep in mind that prices change, and the economics of processing fish should be reviewed from time to time.

But assuming you do wish to process the fish you have caught or have come by some other way, what are the earmarks of a good quality fish? Look for eyes that are bright and clear, flesh that is firm to the touch, and gills pink to red in color. And be certain that no unpleasant odors emanate from it.

Preparing Fish for Processing

We have not yet discussed the matter of slaughter and eviscerating animals except wild game. We have instead assumed that animals had already been properly slaughtered and cleaned either on the farm or in a commercial slaughterhouse. Since, like game, fish is so perishable, it usually befalls the fisherman to clean his catch as soon as it is caught (entrails must be removed a maximum of two hours after catch). For this reason we shall give below steps* for cleaning and preparing for processing.

1 **Fin fish.**
  - Wash and remove scales if any by scraping gently from the tail to the head with a dull edge of a knife, or better still, with a common spoon, which prevents scales from spattering about.
  - Remove entrails after cutting the entire length of the belly from the vent to the head. Remove the head by cutting above the collarbone and then breaking the backbone over the edge of the cutting board or table.
  - Remove the dorsal or large back fin by cutting the flesh along each side, and pulling the fin out. Never trim the fins off with shears or a knife because the bones at the base of the fin will be left in the flesh.
  - Wash the fish thoroughly in cold running water. The fish is now dressed or pan-dressed, depending on its size.

*Based largely on USDA Home and Garden Bulletin No. 93

- It is also possible to skin the fish instead of scaling it after the entrails have been removed and it has been beheaded and de-finned. To do this, run very hot water over the outside of the fish for 45 seconds or so; the skin is then easily pulled off from the flesh. Or dunk the fish in slightly boiling water for a few seconds; then skin it.
- Save the roe for canning or freezing.
- Large dressed fish may be cut cross-wise into steaks, usually about ¾ inch thick.
- To fillet: with a sharp knife, cut down the back of the fish from the tail to the head. Then cut down into the backbone just above the collarbone. Turn the knife flat and cut the flesh along the backbone to the tail, allowing the knife to run over the rib bones. Lift off the entire side of the fish in one piece, freeing the fillet at the tail. Turn the fish over and cut the fillet from the other side.
- If you have not already skinned the fish and wish to skin the fillets, lay the fillet flat on the cutting board, skin side down. Hold the tail end with your fingers, and cut through the flesh to the skin. Flatten the knife on the skin and cut the flesh away from the skin by running the knife forward while holding the free end of the skin firmly between your fingers.

2 **Shellfish.** There are basically two kinds of shellfish: bivalves (clams, oysters, and scallops, for example, which have shells hinged together) and crustaceans (such as lobsters, crabs, and crayfish).

- Bivalves. These should be washed in a mild salt solution (⅔ cup of salt to a gallon of pure water) to remove dirt. They are then shucked or shelled, and the best method of preserving is freezing. Natural juices from the bivalves may be saved and used instead of brine to cover the meat if it is to be frozen in glass jars or in rigid containers.

- Crustaceans. They should be put live into boiling water or a mild brine solution ($^2/_3$ cup salt in a gallon of pure water) and cooked about fifteen minutes, after which the viscera are removed and the shells broken to remove the meat.

It is well to remember that small fish spoil more quickly than large fish, and fat fish (i.e. mackerel, flounder, lake trout) spoil more quickly than lean fish (i.e. cod, perch, coho). Never use shellfish from contaminated water, or off-season when "red tide" may be a problem.

Freezing Fin Fish
Non-shell fish may be prepared in several forms for freezing: 1. **whole,** just caught; 2. **drawn,** which is similar to whole except that the fish has been eviscerated; 3. **dressed or pan-dressed,** which means the fish has had its scales, entrails, and probably its head, tail, and fins removed; 4. **as steaks,** which means that large dressed fish were cut into cross-sections; and 5. **fillets,** or sides of fish cut lengthwise and away from the backbone.

Figure 11-1 illustrates those various forms of preparation.

Large fish are ususally cut into steaks or fillets, while it is more common for small fish to be drawn or pan-dressed for freezing.

But whatever your choice of preparation, be certain that no time is lost after the fish are caught to have them frozen, if that is your intention. Until they are given the fast-freeze, they should be kept chilled (as close to 32° F without freezing as possible).

And as we have said so many times, you get top quality from freezing only when you start with top quality meat.

The following table* indicates the approximate yield of edible portions of fish when prepared according to one of these five basic styles. It is quite clear from the table that fillets are 100% edible, and therefore the space they occupy in your freezer is 100% efficient - no waste at all. Compare that with freezing a whole fish, in which case only 45% of it is edible. So,

*USDA Home and Garden Bulletin No. 93

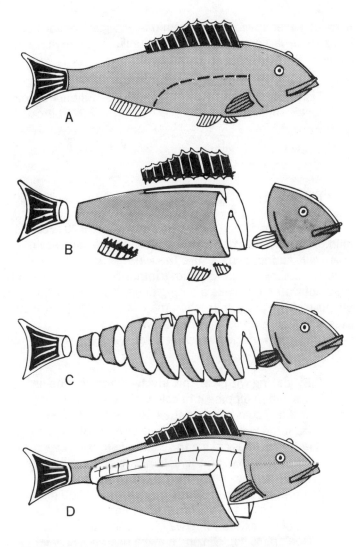

Alternate ways to prepare fish for freezing.
(A) Drawn fish after removal of entrails. (B) Dressed
fish showing removal of fins, head and tail. (C) Fish
cut for steaks. Fish best suited for steaks are large
and fleshy. (D) Fish cut for fillets — cut to remove
nearly all bone.

Figure 11-1

if your freezer space is at a premium, you may well decide to
freeze your large fish as fillets and steaks, the most efficient
ways.

Fish Yields (approximate)	**Edible Portion** (percent)
Whole	45
Drawn	48
Dressed or pan-dressed	67
Steaks	84
Fillets	100

Before fish is frozen, it is well to dip it for 20-30 seconds in a
mild brine solution. Use a good grade of pure salt with no
chemicals added, and be sure the water is pure even if it
requires boiling it first to remove impurities. ⅔ cup of salt to a
gallon of water will make a strong enough brine solution. The
purpose of the dip is to freshen the fish and also to prevent
excess dripping when it is later thawed.

You may now decide which of three ways you wish to freeze
your fish:

1 **By glazing with ice.** This involves freezing the fish
   first; then dipping it in cold water, which will
   create a coat of ice on the fish as it is withdrawn
   from the water. Three or four dips should make a
   good thickness of ice to seal the fish. It is not
   necessary to wrap the fish; however you will need
   to check it every few weeks to see if the ice has
   chipped off and requires more icing. Or you may
   decide to wrap the glazed fish in moisture-vapor-
   proof paper the same way you would wrap meat
   (see pp. 46-48). Glazing may be used not only for
   whole fish, but also for dressed or drawn fish and
   even for chunks. Glazing reduces freezer burn and
   delays rancidity.
2 **By wrapping in moisture-vapor-proof paper
   without glazing.** This is fast and simple. Be guided
   by the instructions in Chapter 3 on Freezing and
   wrap as you would wrap meat. Double layers of

wax paper should be used between steaks and small fillets to make them easier to separate when thawing.

3 **By freezing in rigid containers.** Small fish, steaks, and fillets are probably easiest to handle in rigid containers. Containers should be filled to within an inch of the top; then a weak brine solution (about ⅓ cup salt to one gallon of pure water) should be poured over the fish to fill all air spaces around the pieces and to come just over the top of the pack, again leaving about an inch of headspace. Seal the containers and fast-freeze them at -10°F or lower and store at 0°F.

Frozen packages should be labeled as to contents, number, and description, such as "Five codfish steaks," and dated. Un-wrapped glazed fish are not so easy to label; so we would suggest noting the appropriate details in a freezer inventory book.

Frozen fin fish will normally store for 6-9 months if stored at 0°F. But the more fat, the less the recommended storage time.

And frozen fish may be cooked either before or after thawing; but remember that if cooked frozen, more time will be required. If fish are to be breaded or fried, they should be thawed first for the sake of convenience. When thawing, keep the fish in their original wrappers and thaw in the refrigerator. Cook them as soon as they have thawed.

Freezing Roe

Roe may be frozen, but it should be frozen very quickly after the fish is caught. Roe spoils exceedingly fast. During the time it is exposed to air, do not let it come in direct sunlight. Clean each set of roe carefull, being sure that dirt, pieces of intestines, and body waste are completely removed. Wash each set in fresh water; then puncture the membrane surrounding each set a few times with a sharp and sterile small point. Each set of roe should be packed in individual plastic bags since they will allow you to push out most of the air surrounding it. Several bags of roe may be placed in a single rigid container, sealed, and fast-frozen at -10°F or below and stored at 0°F.

Frozen roe should be consumed within three months.

Freezing Shellfish

Freezing shellfish requires somewhat more preparation than is usually required with fin fish. Oysters, scallops, and clams should first be washed either in pure water or in a weak brine of ⅓ cup of salt to a gallon of pure water. They are then shucked and packed in rigid containers to within an inch of the top. Weak brine, or a combination of brine and their natural juices (which you saved while they were being shucked) may be poured to within an inch of the top of the pack. Then the container should be sealed, labeled, and fast-frozen at a temperature of -10°F or below.

Shrimp may be frozen either cooked or raw; and, if raw, either shucked or not. They, too, should be washed, and then have their heads removed. If they are shucked, the dark vein should be removed. They should then be packed in rigid containers. If they are packed without shucking, the container may be filled to the top; if however shucked but uncooked, they may be packed to within an inch of the top in a rigid container and then covered with mild brine solution to remove all air, sealed, and fast-frozen.

When shrimp are cooked before freezing, they are usually boiled in lightly salted water for approximately 10 minutes as soon as their heads are removed. Then they are shucked, the dark vein is removed, and they are fast-frozen in a sealed rigid container packed to the top.

Crabs and lobsters should be plunged into boiling water, or very mild brine, for 10 to 20 minutes, after which the meat is removed from the claws, tail, and body and packed in rigid containers to within a half-inch of the top. No brine or other liquid is required, although a mild brine may be used if desired. Seal and fast-freeze as directed for other fish products.

Maximum recommended storage time for shellfish in a freezer at 0°F is from 4 to 6 months.

Canning Fish

If we had to cast a vote in preference to either canned or frozen fish, we would vote for frozen. For some reason frozen fish seems to hold the freshness considerably better than in cans. However canned fish has a much longer storage period than frozen fish products have. Furthermore there are many people who do not have their own freezers, and community freezer lockers are not always available. And finally, there is really nothing wrong with canned fish!

We shall not endeavor to present instructions for all kinds of fish products that may be canned; we shall, instead, give instructions for certain kinds, leaving it up to you to determine which best fits your needs. But if any questions persist, contact your local County Extension Agent for additional information, or check one of the numerous recipe or canning books on the market for instructions. A few recipes for canning fish products appear in Chapter 13.

Two things to keep in mind: it is not necessary to remove the bones when canning, for bones frequently add to the flavor of canned fish; and always use either pint glass jars or No. 2 plain tin cans. The larger sizes are not recommended. (C-enamel cans may also be used for seafood.)

Fin Fish

For basic preparation, the fins and scales, if any, should be removed as well as the heads, and the fish should be eviscerated, cleaned, and washed. The backbone should remain intact. The flesh should be cut into pieces the length of your canning jar or tin can, and these pieces should then be soaked for an hour in a brine solution of half a pound of salt to one gallon of pure water. Then drain and pack the pieces of fish into containers. With very small fish, or with head and tailpieces, considerable space may be saved when packing the containers by alternating head and tailpieces or by alternating small fish headpiece up, then tailpiece up.

1 **Mackerel, lake trout, whitefish,** and **mullet.** And this pertains also to fresh-water fish in general.

Pack the containers fairly tightly, skin-side out, to the top. Submerge them in brine (4 ounces of salt to one gallon of pure water) allowing the brine to cover the open containers. Let the brine boil for 15-20 minutes; then remove the containers, turning them upside down on a wire mesh or rack to drain for a few minutes. Discard the drained liquid. You may then add a couple bay leaves or a small onion if you wish. Seal the containers with their lids, and process in a pressure canner at 10 pounds pressure (240°F) as follows:

- In pint glass jars ....100 minutes
- In No. 2 tin cans................90 minutes

Thirty-five pounds of fresh fish will give you about 12 pints of canned fish.

Many people prefer their mackerel in tomato sauce. If this is your preference, too, once the containers have been drained, pour hot tomato sauce to within a half-inch of the top of the glass container and to the very top of tin cans; then seal and process as above.

2 **Salmon and shad.**

Pack the containers reasonably tight right to the tops.

- In pint glass jars. Adjust jar lids. Seal. Process in a pressure canner at 10 pounds pressure (240°F) for 100 minutes.
- In No. 2 tin cans. Cans should be exhausted; then sealed and processed in a pressure canner at 10 pounds pressure (240°F) for 90 minutes.

Approximately 25 pounds of fresh fish will fill a dozen pint glass jars.

3 **Salt water fin fish.**

   Usually it is best to fillet salt water fish if they are of good size. Fillets should be soaked for about 15 minutes in a brine of 1⅓ cups of salt to a gallon of pure water. After draining, fillets should be packed in containers to within one inch of the top of glass jars and to the top of tin cans. Without covering the glass jars or tin cans, place them in a pressure canner and steam them for 20 minutes at 10 pounds pressure (240°F). When pressure has returned to zero, remove the containers, inverting them on a wire rack to drain for 2 or 3 minutes. Add a couple tablespoons of salad, vegetable, or olive oil to each container, seal, and process in a pressure canner at 10 pounds pressure (240°F) as follows:

   - In pint glass jars ....100 minutes
   - In No. 2 tin cans.................90 minutes

4 **River herring.**

   Soak the cleaned herring for six hours in a strong brine solution (about 4 cups of salt in a gallon of pure water should be adequate). However, if the skin starts to wrinkle or change color, remove the fish without waiting for the six-hour period to be up. Fish should be cut into pieces of proper length to fit your glass jars or tin cans, and alternating head and tailpieces when filling them will save space. Fill all remaining space in containers with a brine made of 1½ tablespoons of salt to 1 quart of pure water, and exhaust containers for 10 minutes (212°F). Tin cans are then sealed, but glass jars have their lids put on but not sealed until after processing.

   Note that with river herring, processing in the pressure canner is at 15 pounds pressure (250°F).

   - In pint glass jars ....70 minutes
   - In No. 2 tin cans ....60 minutes

25 pounds of freshly caught fish should fill about 12 pint jars or No. 2 cans.

5 **River herring roe.**

Be sure roe is meticulously clean with no remnants of viscera, blood, or black skin remaining. Wash it in pure water and spread it thinly on a wire mesh to drain for about ten minutes. Roe has a tendency to swell when being processed; so it is best to fill the containers by weighing the roe: 14 ounces will be about right for a pint glass jar or a No. 2 can. Otherwise leave ¾ inch of head space. Make a brine of 2 tablespoons salt to 1 quart of pure water and fill containers to top.

- In pint glass jars. Adjust lids but do not seal tightly until after processing 70 minutes at 15 pounds pressure in a pressure canner (250°F).
- In No. 2 tin cans. Exhaust for 8 minutes at boiling temperature (212°F). Seal, and process 60 minutes at 15 pounds pressure (250°F) in a pressure canner. 10 pounds of roe should fill 12 pint glass jars or the same number of No. 2 cans.

6 **Other kinds of roe.**

Proceed as with river herring roe to clean it meticulously and wash it in pure fresh water. After slitting the membrane covering each section of roe, separate it from the membrane; this may be accomplished by pushing the roe through a raised one-eighth-inch screen grid or by putting everything through a meat grinder having one-eighth inch, or slightly larger, holes, after which the membrane may be removed from the roe.

Stir roe in a brine made of 2 tablespoons of salt to one quart of pure water. You will need 3 pints for each 5 pounds of roe.

Then continue as if you were canning river herring roe.

Shellfish

1 **Clams.**

Clams should be scrubbed clean, then steamed and opened. Be certain to save the juice. Put the clam meat into a weak brine solution of ⅓ cup salt to 1 gallon of pure water and wash well. Boil it for two minutes in a solution of ½ teaspoon of citric acid to one gallon of pure water. After draining, pack the clams into glass jars or tin cans, leaving 1 inch of head space. Cover with juice left over from steaming, but, if necessary, boiling water may be used to fill the jars to within an inch of the top and the tin cans up to the top. Seal and process in a pressure canner at 10 pounds pressure (240°F) as follows:

- In pint glass jars ....70 minutes
- In No. 2 tin cans.................60 minutes

2 **Crab meat.**

Crabs, if dunked in ice-cold water for five minutes, become lethargic; then they should be killed - best done with a knife. Legs and claws should be pulled off as well as the back shell. Discard all viscera and inedible parts and wash thoroughly in pure water. Boil for 20 minutes in a solution of 1 gallon of pure water, 1 cup of salt, and either ¼ cup of white vinegar or lemon juice. Drain, remove meat from the shells and claws, and rinse in a new brine of 1 gallon of pure water and 1 cup of salt. Let drain and rinse again in a solution of 1 gallon of pure water and 1 cup of vinegar. Put the meat in cheesecloth or a bag of similar material and squeeze out excess liquid. Then pack it in pint glass jars or in No. 2 tin cans.

- In pint glass jars. Fill to within an inch of the top, add boiling water to cover the meat only, seal,

and process in a pressure canner at 5 pounds pressure (228°F) for 100 minutes.
- In No. 2 tin cans. If you wish, you may line the cans with vegetable parchment to protect the meat from possible discoloration from the metal. Fill cans to top with meat, and with boiling water. Exhaust cans, seal, and process in a pressure canner at 5 pounds pressure (228°F) for 95 minutes.

3 **Shrimp.**

Shrimp are very perishable; so work swiftly once they have been caught.

Give them a good washing, then drain and boil for 10 minutes in a brine made of 1 cup salt to 1 gallon of pure water and 1 cup of white vinegar. Cool in cold water before peeling off the shell and taking out the black sand vein. After another rinse in cold water, they may be packed as follows:

- In pint glass jars. Leave one inch of headspace and cover with boiling water, still leaving one inch of headspace. Seal and process in a pressure canner at 5 pounds pressure (228°F) for for 45 minutes.
- In No. 2 tin cans. Pack to top and fill to top with boiling water. Seal and process in a pressure canner at 10 pounds pressure (240°F) for 40 minutes.

The above instructions for canning fish give some indication of the various ways it may be done, depending whether fin fish or shellfish, and whether fat fish or lean. To cover every type of fish, to include all fish products such as smoked and pickled fish, chowders, etc. would add little to what has already been said. Canning instructions for specific fish and recipes are found in the many cook books, government publications, and booklets from makers of canning equipment that are so easy to come by. Should any questions remain, you would be well advised to check with your local County Extension Agent for help.

Curing Fish

Chapter 4 on Curing should be reviewed.

Fish may be cured either by dry curing or by brine curing. But remember that fatty fish do not cure so well as the leaner types. We do not use saltpeter when curing fish, and we recommend the use of finely ground salt but not iodized salt.

Dry Curing

Fish should be cleaned and dressed so the collarbone remains since it holds the flesh together and provides a way to hang the fish during drying.

When cleaned, fish are usually cut into fillets or else cut along the backbone from the inside and spread open. They should then be washed well in a mild salt solution of 1 cup of salt to one gallon of pure water.

Inspect to be sure that all foreign matter is removed and blood no longer appears anywhere. Then drain for fifteen minutes or so and dredge the fish in salt. If you have a box or some other container with holes in the bottom to allow drainage, use that, piling fish flesh side up in stacks. The top piece is laid flesh side down. When stacking fish, be sure to sprinkle salt generously between the layers as well as under the bottom layer and on top of the top layer. Usually you should figure on about one pound of salt for each four pounds of fish.

Weather dictates considerably how long fish should remain in the dry cure. With good, cool weather, up to a week might be enough; with real warm weather, possibly a couple days would suffice. Some consideration has to be given to the size and thickness of the fish, too, and experimentation is about the only way one is going to find out.

Fish should next be removed from the salt, scrubbed to remove all residue of salt, and dried on racks in the shade. A common type of rack is made of mesh wire stretched over a wooden frame, all this supported well off the ground and shaded by a simple pitched board roof.

Lay the fish out, skin side down, but turn it frequently to be certain it is drying out thoroughly and evenly. Should dew occur at night, or should there be damp weather, stack the fish inside and above the floor. Should foul weather persist for any appreciable length of time, re-pile the fish daily and sprinkle salt between the layers.

The best-known test for how long fish should dry is to squeeze it between your thumb and forefinger. If it is firm and leaves no dent, it is time to wrap the pieces individually in wax paper, place in a wooden box with a tight cover, and store in a cool, dry place.

Brine Curing

A brine cure usually results in a slightly milder cure than a dry cure. Fish with spines and big fins are frequently skinned or scaled; small fish are generally cut down the back but not in two, and spread open in one piece; large fish become fillets with their collarbones attached.

With the brine cure, it is desirable to score thick pieces of fish by making cuts about a half inch deep into, but not through, the flesh, and repeating this about every couple inches. These provide deeper penetration for the brine solution.

After washing the fish and allowing it to soak a half hour in a weak salt solution (½ cup salt to 1 gallon of pure water), it may be drained; then it is dredged in finely ground salt with particular attention being given to pushing salt into the scored areas.

Fish is then stacked in a crock, skin side down. Sprinkle salt first on the bottom of the crock, and on each layer of fish. Fish should be staggered over each previous layer so salt will have maximum advantage to penetrate all parts of the flesh. You will need about one pound of salt for each three pounds of fish, but don't try to overdo on salt. Brine will form automatically.

If the weather is fair, you should be able to remove the fish from the salt after a couple days' curing. But if stormy weather prevails, it may need to stay in the dry salt for up to a week. Only experience can give you the best indication of required time.

Remove and scrub the fish in a strong brine solution (1½ cups of salt to 1 gallon of pure water) and repack in the crock with a saturated solution (4 pounds of salt to 6 quarts of pure water) after sprinkling salt lightly between the layers.

Keep the crock in a cool, dark place, and mark your calendar to change the brine in about three months, or sooner if warm weather causes fermentation to begin.

Maximum storage time for brine-cured fish is about 9-10 months.

Smoking Fish

It would be good to reveiw Chapter 5, which deals with smoking.

Fish may be prepared for smoking either as drawn fish or as fillets. And quite often large fish are cut into steaks. Opening the fish by splitting along the back but not cutting the belly portion makes it simple to spread the fish open to hang in the smoke chamber. As with drying, if the collarbone has not been removed, it is quite easy to hang fish in the smoke chamber on s-hooks.

When brining and smoking fish, you have best results if you confine your activities to one particular kind of fish at a time. And even better results if your fish are nearly all the same size.

Fish, when ready, should be submerged in brine for 12 hours and held to a temperature of 38°F-40°F. The brine solution should be 1½ cups of salt for each gallon of pure water; this amount is good for about four pounds of fish.

After brining, fish should be removed and drained. Then rinsed to be sure that all accumulated salt is removed. To be certain that air can circulate all around them, it is best to dry them on s-hooks through the gill or under the collarbone, or to lay them skin-down on a wire mesh. The first way is the better, and if the bony collar has been left on the fillets, it should be quite easy to hang fish on s-hooks to dry. Furthermore during smoking the collarbone becomes support to hold the flesh together. Fillets with skin removed may be spread over three-sided wooden rods or even nailed to dowels.

Rather than brining the fish for 12 hours, some prefer

leaving fish in brine only thirty minutes or so to remove any remaining blood or other impurities, then packing them in dry salt for 1 to 12 hours, following which time they are rinsed and dried.

The drying operation is most important; for a thin, glossy sheen will develop on fish that is dried properly - a sort of skin-like film known as the "pellicle." It may take up to three hours of drying for this to appear; but unless it does form, the smoking process will result in irregular and unappetizing pieces of fish covered with white curd. But a good pellicle will result in a smooth and attractive surface for the smoke, and it will help secure the juices during the smoking process.

And, a reminder, fish must always be dried in the shade. Direct sun will cause almost immediate spoilage.

Once the pellicle is formed, the fish is ready for the smoke chamber where it should be hung on dowels, s-hooks, split and hung on rods, or placed on wire mesh racks. The wire racks, if used, should first be coated with cooking oil so the fish will not become stuck during the smoking process.

For cold smoking the temperature of the smoke should stay at 70°F or under.

The longer fish is smoked, the longer it may be stored without deterioration. If you plan to store for only a couple weeks, you will surely need to smoke if for twenty-four hours right around the clock without stopping. But it may be smoked even longer for longer storage; it is conceivable you might wish to smoke for a couple or more weeks. Much depends on the type of fish, the degree of smoking you find preferable to your taste, the depth of smoke color you desire, and to some extent the way your fish has been prepared (whole, dressed, fillets, steaks). So there is plenty of room for experimentation toward self-satisfaction.

Because fish is extremely perishable, once the smoking process has begun, it should be completed without interruption. This means you should be prepared to smoke day and night until you have decided that the fish is completely smoked to your liking.

When smoking is completed and the fish is completely cooled, it should be removed and packaged for storage similarly

Air-Drying

Because of so many uncontrollable variables, we do not recommend drying fish in the open air. Yet we are aware that people in some sections of the country do it successfully. It still is not done on a large scale. Other methods of storing fish and fish products are so successful and so easy to do without worrying about all these variables that we suggest if anyone wishes to air-dry fish, he contact the U.S. Bureau of Fisheries, Washington, D.C. for instructions for his particular geographic area.

Pickling

Practically any kind of fin or shellfish may be pickled in the home. However there are some variables with pickling, too, such as: the acid content of the vinegar, the kind of vinegar (distilled is the recommended kind), the variety of fish, and temperature at which pickled fish may be stored.

Because of all these variables, and because pickling is itself a variation of the curing process, we have chosen not to go into detail on pickling but to suggest instead that you check with the many books that give specific recipes for pickling.

SUGGESTED ADDITIONAL READING

A good library is essential for the person or family raising and storing food. No one can remember all of the information this requires, and a good library will provide it, at your fingertips. New ideas, techniques and theories are always being put forth, and the best way to keep up with them all is to keep your library up to date. There are many good books available; here are some that are excellent choices.

Raising Rabbits the Modern Way, Revised Edition, by Robert Bennett. Everything for the home and commercial producer, 160 pp. illus. $8.95. Order #479-4.

The Family Cow, by Dirk van Loon. Covers cow buying, handling, housing, feeding, milking, caring, breeding, and calfing. Plus information on land use, hay and tools, 272 pp. illus. $8.95. Order # 066-7.

Raising Poultry the Modern Way, by Leonard Mercia. In addition to stock selection, brooding, rearing and more, you are given methods of disease prevention and treatment for laying flock, meat chickens, turkeys, ducks and geese. 240 pp. illus. $8.95. Order #058-6.

Zucchini Cookbook. At last — Nancy Ralston & Marynor Jordan describe wonderful things to do with zucchini! Everything from zucchini marmalade to zucchini raisin pie with over 240 recipes. $6.95. Order #107-8.

Raising Your Own Turkeys, by Leonard Mercia. Complete how-to information on raising turkeys, from young poults to delicious, thick-breasted birds. 160 pp. illus. $6.95. Order # 253-8.

Down-to-Earth Vegetable Gardening Know-How, by Dick Raymond. Learn how to double even triple your yield. A treasury of vegetable gardening information. 144 pp. charts, photos, & illus. $7.95. Order #271-6.

These books are available at your bookstore, lawn & garden center, or may be ordered directly from Garden Way Publishing, Dept. 8900, Schoolhouse Road, Pownal, VT 05261. Include $2.50 per order for Fourth Class Mail, $4.00 for UPS. Send for our free mail order catalog.

12
RECIPES

Whenever one becomes involved with any aspect of food, one encounters recipes from many sources. Often these recipes do not vary a great deal; yet they are quite different, for some small but important change has been made which left the imprint of a creative person. This change may have improved the flavor or added to the succulence of a particular kind of food. How often have we heard a person say, "Did you ever have any of Carol's pickles?" or "Margot makes the best oatmeal cookies I have ever tasted."

Wines, cheeses, and breads become trademarks of the particular country you visit. Certain vintages, varieties, and recipes for them are passed down through the years to become almost a part of the national history. And this is true of meats, especially of cured meats.

Diaries and history books frequently record how a person preserved some kind of food to provide for future needs. An illustration is the following from a book titled Peacham, The Story of a Vermont Hill Town,* which states:

> "'A recipe for salt brine, sufficient for 90 pounds' found in an old account book of John Ewell's (born 1827) describes this process.
>
> Take 9 gal. of soft water 9 pounds of good salt, 3 lbs of brown sugar and 3 oz. of saltpeter boil all well together. Skim often when cold add one oz sodia pack the meat close in the tub then pour on the brine prevent the meat from raising in the tub

*by Ernest L. Bogart © 1948 By The Vermont Historical Society, Montpelier.

by some weight let it remain in the tub until salted through then smoke if pork bacon or dry if beef and it is excellent."

And like wine, cheese and bread, recipes for cured meats are often passed from one generation to another over a hundred and fifty years or more. And these particular ones, because of their excellence, become hallmarks of the families that pass them on.

This chapter includes a number of recipes for meat and meat products primarily to provide guidance in the preparation of them. A number have been taken from government publications because they are good basic recipes. But others have been included because they are variations of good basic recipes - they represent how a recipe may have alterations by a creative person, almost the way a musical theme may have a new arrangement, to provide a recipe that does, indeed, become one worthy of being passed down from one generation to another.

It is hoped, then, that this chapter will show you how simple it is to cater to one's own individual taste in preparing meat until you arrive at something different and distinctive - something that is "you." So don't be afraid to exercise your imagination and try some variation of your own; you will find this fun and rewarding providing you keep in mind the basic things we have discussed in preceding chapters that are required to assure high quality products.

Remember, too, that the ingredients may be reduced or increased proportionately should you prefer to reduce or increase the yield.

DRIED BEEF

Dried beef is made from the heavier-muscled cuts, especially the round. Cut the muscles lengthwise or prepare as a whole muscle. The curing procedure is the same as that used for corned beef except that you may add an extra pound of sugar for each 100 pounds of meat. After the meat is cured, remove it from the

brine, wash, and hang up to dry for 24 hours. Smoke*
the cured meat in the regular manner at a
temperature of 130° F to 140° F for 70 to 80 hours or
until quite dry. The dried beef is ready to be used or
it may be hung in a dry, dark room or wrapped and
hung up for storage. Dried beef is usually cut very
thin for use.

From USDA Farmers' Bulletin No. 2209

DRIED BEEF
200 pounds good fresh-killed beef (the rounds)
1 pint fine salt
¼ pound brown sugar
1 teaspoon saltpeter
   Mix last 3 ingredients well, rubbing out all lumps.
Divide mixture into 3 equal portions. Place meat in
large crocks and rub thoroughly with one portion of
above mixture. Let stand 1 day. Follow same
procedure on second and third days. Turn meat
several times a day. Allow meat to remain in crocks 7
more days, then hang in warm place until meat stops
dripping. When dripping has stopped, hang in cool
shed about 6 weeks to dry thoroughly. Wrap meat in
clean muslin bags and keep in cool place. If in 6
months meat becomes too hard, soak it in cold water
24 hours and wipe dry. Wrap again in muslin bags
and hang in cool place.

From "Pennsylvania Dutch Original Meat Preparations,"
distributed by Dutchcraft Company, Gettysburg, Pa.
Copyright 1964.

---

*Note that this recipe requires smoke hot enough to cook the meat; so control
your fire accordingly, being careful that the meat does not catch fire. You may
wish to have your fire pit built almost directly under the smoke chamber for this
recipe.

JERKY

Jerky is dried meat - usually from beef, lamb, venison or other game. Mountain climbers, hunters, and the pioneers have used it throughout history. And it is quite widely used today since it is light and easy to carry, it does not spoil easily, and it provides energy when needed.

There are many ways to make jerky: some with brine and some without; some with seasonings and herbs, and some without; and some by drying in the sun, and some by drying over coals. If you ask ten people how to make jerky, you could easily have ten different replies.

But bear in mind these facts about jerky: whatever method is used to make it, it should originate from lean meat; it should be dried thoroughly until all moisture has been extracted from it; it should not be cooked; and it should be wrapped in moisture-vapor-proof paper for storage.

One recipe from among the many possible ones is the following:

Cut the lean meat into fairly thin (1 inch) and narrow (1 to 1½ inches) strips of about any length you wish. Soak them in brine (1 cup salt to 1 gallon of pure water) for a couple days. Remove from container and dry. Next hang the strips directly over hot coals made from hard wood. The strips may be stretched over a dowel or a branch supported by forked sticks. Be sure the fire does not flame to burn or cook the meat; it must be hot, but not hot enough to cook - only to provide heat to dry the strips. When the strips are so dry they are brittle when cooled, they are done. And you may wrap them for storage. If your fancy requires some seasoning, rub seasoning or spices well into the meat after brining and before it is hung to dry over the coals.

PEMMICAN

This is a more highly nutritious dehydrated food than jerky, and, again, there are a number of ways it may be made. Even the Indians, who are reputed to have first made it, used several variations.

Lean meat from beef, venison, and other game animals is cut into thin narrow strips and allowed to dry in the sun, over a bed of hot coals, or in an oven with the door open.

The strips are hung on dowels or poles suspended over forked sticks for support. Or they may be draped over a metal rack if dried in the oven.

When the strips are brittle-dry (not cooked), they should be beaten into small pieces of powder; or it might be more simple to run them through a food chopper. Enough hot fat is added to bind the powdered meat and make it almost pasty. Dried fruit (cherries, apples, raisins, currants, for example) and nuts are kneaded into it.

Store in an air-tight container where it is cool and dry, and this will last a long, long time.

VENISON MINCEMEAT

2 pounds of ground venison

2 cups of boiling water

1 pound of ground beef suet

4 pints of peeled and
chopped apples

1 pound of currants

2 pounds of seedless raisins

½ pound of citron

2 pounds of sugar (use 1 cup brown and
3 of white if desired)

5 cups of apple cider

1 teaspoon salt

2 teaspoons cinnamon

1 teaspoon nutmeg

1 teaspoon ground
cloves

Juice of 1 lemon

Cook meat in the 2 cups of boiling water for 1½ hours. Add suet and apples to the cooked venison and cook slowly until the apples are tender; this will be about 45 minutes. Add the remaining ingredients, and simmer until thick. Pack hot into hot sterilized jars. Process pints and quarts for 20 minutes at 10 pounds pressure (240° F). This makes about 4 quarts.

Compiled by Shirley and Anna Wilson, Cooperative Extension Work in Agriculture and Home Economics, State of Vermont, College of Agriculture and Home Economics, University of Vermont and USDA cooperating.

CORNED BEEF

Corned beef is generally made from the cheaper cuts and those that have considerable fat, such as the plate, rump, and chuck.

Remove all bone from the cut and, to facilitate packing, cut pieces into uniform thickness and size. For each 100 pounds of meat, use 8 to 10 pounds of coarse salt. Spread a layer of salt on the bottom of a clean, sterilized wooden barrel or stone crock. Next, pack a layer of meat, sprinkle with salt and add the next layer of meat and salt, and so on. Lightly rub each piece of meat with salt before packing. Allow the packed meat to stand for about 24 hours, at which time cover with a brine made up as follows: for each 100 pounds of meat, use 4 pounds of sugar, 4 ounces of saltpeter and 2 ounces of baking soda dissolved in 4 gallons of water. After covering with brine, weight the meat down.

USDA Farmers' Bulletin No. 2209

CORNED BEEF MADE IN THE REFRIGERATOR

1 quart water
½ cup plus 2 tablespoons salt
⅓ cup light brown sugar
1 teaspoon saltpeter

1 bay leaf
2 whole allspice
2 whole cloves
3 peppercorns

Make enough to cover the piece of beef you have selected and soak it in the refrigerator about 2 weeks. Keep the beef submerged at all times by placing a weight on it. Every two days turn it over in the brine to be sure that it is being cured throughout evenly and thoroughly.

CORNED BEEF

This recipe has been handed down for at least five generations.

For 100 pounds of meat   *3 pounds of brown sugar*
9 pounds of coarse salt   *2 ounces of saltpeter*
½ pint of molasses   *5 gallons of water*

    Boil water and other ingredients, skim. Cool and pour over meat. Weight so meat is kept below surface of liquid.

CURED TONGUE

    Use a cure similar to what you would use for corned beef. Pork tongue usually requires at least 10 days or slightly more for proper curing; beef tongues will need four weeks in the cure. Two weeks should be sufficient for veal tongues.

    Once tongues are cured, scrubbed, and dried, they may be removed to the smokehouse for cold smoking until they achieve the color you desire. Or they may be eaten without being smoked.

BACON

*You may use your favorite ham cure for bacon;
however the length of time required to cure bacon is
less than for ham. For a dry cure, allow bacon strips
to remain in the cure about 1½ days per pound. For a
sweet pickle cure, 2 days or slightly less per pound are
usually sufficient.*

*Remember that these curing times are only
estimates; experience will tell you whether to increase
or decrease the length of time needed.*

BEEF BACON

*For beef bacon, follow the recipe for pork bacon,
using instead rolled boneless blades. Or you may vary
the cure by using the cure for pastrami.*

*This should be smoked at 130°F - 140°F until dry
and hard.*

CANADIAN BACON

*For this very delicious processed meat, use the pork
loin, curing it with your favorite sweet pickle as you
would for ordinary bacon. Then smoke to your taste.*

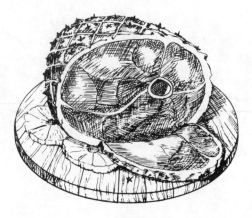

HAMS

The following recipe for smoked hams from the "Cracker Barrel Cook Book"* is a beautiful example of the way many recipes are handed down from one generation to another. The notes and comments that go along with the ingredients spell out the important directions for making a ham that has become a choice and respected delicacy over the years. This is quite typical of many that are found in family cookbooks, and such are indeed a credit to those who have passed the recipes along.

For every hundred pounds of meat, take five pints of good molasses, (or five pounds of brown sugar) five ounces of saltpeter, and eight pounds of rock salt - add three gallons of water, and boil the ingredients over a gentle fire, skimming off the scum as it arises. Continue the boiling till the salt, etc. is dissolved. Have the hams, nicely cut and trimmed, packed in casks with the shank-end down, as the pickle will thus strike in better. When the pickle, prepared as above, is sufficiently cool, pour it over the hams. They may lie in pickle from two to six weeks, according to the size of the pieces or the state of the weather, more time

---

*"Cracker Barrel Cook Book" by Ladies Aid of the First Congregational Church, Newbury, Vermont© 1957 C.H. Stamm.

being required in cold than in warm weather. Much
of the goodness of hams depends on the smoking.
They should be hung up with the shank end
downwards, as this will prevent the escape of their
juices by dripping. Small hams, wanted for immediate
use, will answer with two weeks smoking; but large
ones, and those wanted for keeping, should be smoked
four weeks or more. Different articles are used for
smoking. Perhaps sawdust from hard wood, where it
can be conveniently had, is, on the whole to be
preferred. Corn-cobs are first rate, and are said by
some to make the 'sweetest' smoke of anything. Chips
of maple and hickory, or small twigs and branches of
those kinds of wood, do well. Another mode which we
have seen practiced is to SMOKE THE BARRELS
OR CASKS in which the hams are kept, and let them
remain in pickle till wanted, only taking them out a
sufficiently long time before using to allow them to
drain properly. The barrels are smoked by being
placed over small fires of chips, cobs, etc., for several
hours. The essence of the smoke which is thus
imbibed by the barrel is imparted to the pickle, and
thence to the meat.

HAM
The following recipe is at least five generations old.

For 100 pounds of meat:

4 gallons of water	*8 pounds of salt*
3 pounds of brown sugar	*3 ounces of saltpeter*

Let simmer on stove, cool and pour over meat. Be
sure there is no blood in meat. Ham will be cured in 6
weeks and ready to be smoked.
  The above pickle may also be used for corned beef.
Corned beef will be ready in 10-14 days.

CURED HAMS,
PENNSYLVANIA DUTCH STYLE

100 pounds ham   *1/8 pound black pepper*
3 ounces saltpeter   *1/2 pound brown sugar*
5 pints fine salt

Use only corn-fed hogs. Mix saltpeter, sugar and 1 pint salt thoroughly, rub over hams (being sure to get plenty in the hock) and let stand 24 hours. Then rub meat with pepper and 2 pints salt. Let stand 5 days, then rub meat again with remaining salt. Set aside 30 days, then hang meat and brush off salt. Have hams smoked 10 days with hickory or apple wood. Rub hams with red pepper, wrap in brown paper, then in muslin bags and hang up, hock down. Hams prepared in this manner will keep indefinitely, and flavor and quality improve with time.

From "Pennsylvania Dutch Original Meat Preparations," distributed by Dutchcraft Company, Gettysburg, Pa. Copyright 1964.

COUNTRY HAM

8 pounds of salt
3 pounds of sugar (white or granulated light brown)
3 ounces of saltpeter

Apply curing mix to the hams as soon as they have chilled and the hams have been dressed. Use 1¼ ounces of curing mix per pound of ham. Rub the mix on ham at three different times: 1st when meat is cut and is ready to go on the shelf*; 2nd on the third day;

---

*Note that a curing shelf is used instead of a curing box or barrel.

and 3rd on the 10th day, or seven days after the second application. Cover all surfaces, but no need to rub the ham a lot with it; but be sure to pack some curing mix in the shank end at each application.

Cure from 36°F to 40°F for the following lengths of time:

> 15 lb. ham stays in cure for 2 days per pound, or 30 days
> 20 lb. ham stays in cure 1¾ days per pound, or 35 days
> 25 lb. ham stays in cure 1½ days per pound, or 38-40 days

Remove from cure and soak in cold water for 1½ to 2 hours to remove surface salt. Dry the hams and store them under refrigeration for 20 to 30 days at which time the salt should be equalized in the hams.

Then smoke at between 70°F and 90°F for two days or until the hams have an amber or mahogany color.

After smoking, hams must go through an aging process to obtain the country-style aged flavor, and care must be taken to prevent insects from invading the stored hams. They must be bagged and hung for 30 days under refrigeration at 40°F - 45°F; then taken out of refrigeration and hung in a temperature of 70°F for about 6 months; a temperature in the 80's is even better. Hams over a year old tend to become hard.

This recipe is based on "Curing Hams Country Style," published by the North Carolina Agricultural Extension Service, State College Station, Raleigh, N.C., January 1971.

MAPLE SUGAR PICKLE FOR HAM

100 pounds of ham	*2 pounds of sugar*
10 gallons of water	*1 quart of maple syrup*
9 pounds of salt	*2 ounces of soda*
2 ounces of salt water	*1 ounce allspice*

Combine ingredients and place in large crocks. Let the meat stay in the pickle for six weeks. Remove and smoke with corn cobs.

Brown sugar may be substituted for the sugar and maple syrup. For 100 pounds of ham about 5 pounds of brown sugar would be needed, however Vermonters feel that the maple syrup gives a better flavor. Some of the natives use the ham simply pickled and not smoked.

Above recipe from "A Vermont Cook Book" by Vermont Cooks, published by the Green Mountain Studios, Inc., White River Junction, Vermont. Copyright 1958 by Green Mountain Studios. This recipe may also be used for pickling bacon preliminary to smoking it.

ARDENNES HAM

This recipe has been in a Belgian family for many years, and it is greatly admired by all who have eaten this ham. You will note that the ham is not cooked before it is eaten; therefore it is important that your pork is of high quality and free from any disease. The recipe is good for 100 pounds of meat.

10 pounds of gray sea salt*
½ heaping teaspoon of Ardennes thyme (or any
   variety of pungent thyme)
¼ heaping teaspoon hysop
1½ sage leaves
1½ bay leaves
1½ bunches of garlic (bunches, not just the cloves)
5 shallots
5 juniper berries
2½ ounces of black pepper freshly ground
½ teaspoon freshly grated nutmeg
½ teaspoon freshly grated cloves
½ teaspoon of a less pungent variety of thyme
½ teaspoon fresh savory (the perennial type)

Mix the herbs together the night before, possibly running them through a grinder; and the following morning mix everything together with the salt. Rub each side of the ham with the curing mix in a kneading motion (rubber gloves may come in handy for this.)

Pack the hams in salt in a wooden barrel with drain holes, or in a crock with a raised bottom to hold the liquid that is drained from the ham by the salt. The cure should last from 8 to 30 days depending on the amount of fat in the ham (the more fat, the longer

---

*Gray sea salt may be ordered from health food stores. Should it not be available, ground rock salt may be used. But be sure salt crystals are not too large - about peppercorn size.

the curing time. Also, the more fat, the less satisfactory will be the ham.) Overhaul as described on pages 58 and 60. When time is up, dry thoroughly and smoke for the same number of days as the ham was cured. Smoking must be around the clock. Maple and birch sawdust is highly recommended to produce the smoke. This must be cold smoke; do not let temperature of the smoke go over 70°F at any time.

Wrap the ham for storage. It should not be eaten for at least one year, and it will be much better if not eaten until it has aged for two years.

When eaten, it is served raw and cold and cut into paper-thin slices. Since it is not cooked, be 100% sure that your ham is healthy and free from any kind of potentially harmful organism before starting the curing process.

This same recipe may be used to cure bacon, which will take about 7 to 10 days in the cure.

Trout, venison, turkey, and beef have also been cured and smoked with this same recipe with excellent results.

FISH CHOWDER

2½ *pounds of cleaned fish*　　½ *cup chopped onions*
1½ *quarts of water*　　　　　4 *cups of diced potatoes*
Salt to taste　　　　　　　　¼ *pound of salt pork*
Pepper to taste

　　*Fish should be cleaned and have all scales, fins,
and the tail removed. Cut fillets into small (one inch)
pieces and keep them refrigerated until needed. Use
the bones for soup stock, boiling until the meat falls
from the bones; season with salt and pepper. Strain
the soup stock. Dice pork and cook it until brown in a
frying pan. Add onions to pork and continue cooking
until they are tender and yellow. Combine all
ingredients including the fish stock, pork and onions,
and fillets. Boil for 10 minutes. Season according to
preference, adding to taste any other seasoning
especially preferred, and pour into glass jars or tin
cans. Seal and process in pressure canner at 10 to 15
pounds pressure (240° F), depending on altitude.*

　　In pint glass jars . . . . *100 minutes*
　　In No. 2 tin cans . . . . *90 minutes*

PICKLED TRIPE

After you have thoroughly cleaned and rinsed the tripe in cold water, scald it in hot water (a little below the boiling point). When sufficiently scalded, remove the inside lining of the stomachs by scraping, which will leave a clean, white surface. Boil tripe until tender (usually about 3 hours) and then place in cold water so that you may scrape the fat from the outside. When you have done this, peel off the membrane from the outside of the stomach, and the clean, white tripe is ready for pickling.

Place the tripe in a clean, hardwood barrel or earthenware jar, and keep submerged in a strong brine for 3 or 4 days. Rinse with cold water and cover with pure cider vinegar or a spiced pickling liquid. Place a weight on the tripe to keep it from floating on the surface of the liquid.

From USDA Farmers' Bulletin No. 2209

PICKLED FISH

Soak 10 pounds of fish in weak brine (1 cup salt to one gallon pure water) for an hour. Drain and pack in a crock in a solution of strong brine (2½ pounds salt to one gallon pure water) for 12 hours. A temperature of 40° F to 50° F should be maintained.

Rinse fish in fresh water. Combine the following ingredients in a large pan or kettle, bring to a boil and add fish:

1 ounce allspice
1 ounce mustard seed or 2 ounces regular mixed pickling spice
½ pound onions, sliced

2 quarts distilled (white) vinegar
½ ounce bay leaves
2½ pints water
1 ounce white pepper
1 ounce hot, ground or dried peppers (optional
and to taste)

Simmer for 10 minutes or until fish is easily pierced with a fork. Remove fish from the liquid and place in a single layer on a flat pan and refrigerate for rapid cooling to prevent spoilage. Pack cold fish in a clean glass jar adding a few spices, a bay leaf, freshly sliced onion, and if desired, a slice of lemon.

Strain the vinegar solution, bring to a boil, and pour into jars until the fish are covered. Seal the container with a new two-part canning lid immediately. This product must be stored in the refrigerator at 40° F - 45° F and should be used within 4 to 6 weeks.

From: "Home Smoking and Pickling of Fish," University of Wisconsin, Sea Grant Program, Cooperative Extension Programs, Madison, Wisconsin.

PICKLED OYSTERS

1 gallon shucked oysters
3 pints oyster liquor
1 pint distilled vinegar
1 pint white wine, dry
2 tablespoons ground onion
2 cloves garlic, crushed
2 tablespoons crushed bay leaves
1 tablespoon chopped parsley stems
1 tablespoon crushed fennel
1 tablespoon crushed allspice
1 tablespoon crushed black peppers
1 tablespoon crushed cloves
1 tablespoon crushed cinnamon
¼ tablespoon crushed mace
¼ tablespoon crushed thyme

*Open one gallon of oysters, saving the liquor.
Strain the liquor and add sufficient salted water to
bring the amount up to 3 pints. Simmer the mixture
gently over a low flame. When the liquor is near the
boiling point, add the oysters a few at a time, cooking
until the "fringe" curls. The oysters are then removed
from the liquor and set aside to cool. Make a sauce of
vinegar, white wine, bay leaves, onion, garlic,
parsley, fennel, thyme, cloves, black pepper, allspice,
cinnamon, and mace. Add this sauce to the oyster
liquor and simmer 30 to 45 minutes. When it is cool,
pack the oysters in glass jars with a bay leaf, slice of
lemon, and a few fresh spices in each jar. Strain the
liquor, and when it is cool pour it into jars, seal
immediately, and store in a cool, dark place. The
oysters are ready to use in 10 to 14 days.*

From Fishery Leaflet 554, U.S. Department of the Interior, Fish
and Wildlife Service, Bureau of Commercial Fisheries.

PASTRAMI

Pastrami knows no limits to the number of herbs and spices that may be used in the cure. Custom and personal preference to a large degree determine what the ingredients will be.

The following is a guide for the simple preparation of pastrami. If you wish to add juniper berries or any number of other spices to the cure, do so. Here is a chance to experiment and come up with some great food eating that bears your personal imprint.

Start with the basic brine for corned beef, adding to it six finely chopped garlic cloves. Beef briskets are best for pastrami. Leave them in this cure for two weeks at 34° F - 40° F; then hang them for a day in a cool dry airy room, after which they should be removed to the smokehouse.

Smoke with hot smoke until a thermometer in the middle of the cured briskets reaches 138° F. You may wish to build your fire fairly close to the bottom of the smoke chamber.

PICKLED BEEF AND PORK

For those who insist that the only pickled meats are those that are pickled with vinegar, recipes may be found in many of the standard cookbooks. But for others, pickling is simply curing with a sweet pickle cure.

While hams, shoulders, bacon strips, and briskets are the most commonly used cuts for sweet pickle cures, they are by no means the only ones. As we have said so many times, it takes only imagination and a bit of daring to venture beyond the usual. One should not be restricted by custom and strict adherence to recipe books from doing the unusual and letting one's imagination have a little exercise. However, and this must be remembered, no short-cuts should ever be taken that will lower the standards for top quality, sanitation, and sound meat products.

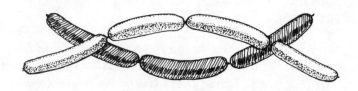

SAUSAGE

This is another recipe that has been handed down for at least five generations.

For 40 pounds of meat - pork and beef mixed, ground fine:

12 ounces salt	*2 ounces pepper*
6 ounces sage	*2 tablespoons ginger*

This uses uniodized salt and home-grown sage - not commercial.

CARL KOENIG'S SAUSAGE

3 pounds beef and pork ground together - in any desired proportion
½ pound coarse chopped salt pork
1 large onion, chopped
2 cloves garlic, crushed
1 teaspoon each of the following:

dried thyme	*ground mustard seed*
dried basil	*chili powder*
ground coriander	*fennel seeds*

salt and pepper as you like it

Mix well, pack into muslin bag (sleeve) and keep refrigerated. Or it may be smoked until dark brown.

The following note from the author of this recipe is interesting, for it indicates how a sausage may reflect one's feelings, and how it provides an opportunity to be creative:

> "Since I cook the way I paint (no two pictures ever the same), my recipes change from one time to the next. I may make the meat equal parts of beef, pork, and veal. The spices certainly change as mood dictates. I believe a cook should be flexible and inventive."

SMOKED SAUSAGE
For 100 pounds pork trimmings use the following:

2 pounds of salt
2 to 4 ounces ground sage
2 to 4 ounces ground black pepper
½ to 1 ounce red pepper if desired
½ to 1 ounce ground cloves, or
1 ounce ground nutmeg if desired
12 ounces of sugar

Thoroughly mix the seasoning, spread it over the trimmings, and grind the whole quantity through a fine plate. You may prefer to grind the unseasoned meat through a plate with ½-inch holes and then mix it with the spices and regrind through a plate with 1/8-inch holes.

If you are stuffing the sausage into casings, do so immediately after grinding. If it is too stiff to stuff properly, add 6 to 10 cups of cold water and knead until the mass becomes doughlike. Stuff tightly in casings and allow to cure for about 24 hours in a cool

*place. Smoke and dry at a temperature of 70°F to
90°F for a day or two until a dark mahogany color is
obtained. Do not keep this sausage until hot weather
unless it is canned.*

From Farmers' Bulletin No. 2138 - with minor adaptations.

LIVERWURST

*Use the trimmings of a pig's head (every single bit
you can get off) and add to this the heart, kidneys,
and any of the other internal organs you do not have
other use for.*

*Now grind all this up, adding to it pork fat in the
amount of your personal preference.*

*Boil the above until soft; then put it through the
grinder along with half the pig's liver, two or three
pounds of onions, spices as you prefer (salt, pepper,
marjoram, for instance). Mix well, stuff into casings,
and smoke if you prefer.*

*If no casings are available, put into a pan, let cool,
cut into portions and freeze.*

LIVER SAUSAGE,
PENNSYLVANIA DUTCH STYLE

35 pounds pork trimmings	*2 ounces sweet marjoram*
15 pounds lean veal or beef	*1 pound salt*
7 pounds dry bread	*1 ounce allspice*
7 pounds liver	*6 cloves garlic if desired*

*Cover pork and veal with water and cook 3 hours.
Drain, saving liquid. Cool and remove bones. Soften
bread with cold water; squeeze dry. Grind meat, liver
and bread very fine. Add 5 quarts meat stock,*

marjoram, salt, allspice and minced garlic. Mix
thoroughly, about 15 minutes. Soak casings in warm
borax solution. Rinse, drain and fill with sausage
mixture. Drop into boiling water and simmer until
sausage floats. Plunge into cold water. Dry and store
in a cold place. Fry to serve. Makes 60 pounds.

From "Pennsylvania Dutch Original Meat Preparations,"
distributed by Dutchcraft Company, Gettysburg, Pa.
Copyright 1964.

BOLOGNA SAUSAGE

The Bologna sausage is made of ground pork and beef mixed
with enough water to give the sausage the desirable fine,
tenacious texture. Commercial firms sometimes grind cracked
ice with warm beef from freshly slaughtered cattle because this
method gives a finer grain to the finished product.

One standard recipe for bologna sausage is as
follows:

60 pounds beef
40 pounds pork trimmings
10 quarts cold water
2 to 2½ pounds salt
1 ounce saltpeter
2 to 4 ounces black pepper
1 to 1½ ounces coriander
1 ounce mace
Onions if desired

Grind the chilled beef trimmings with 19 ounces
of salt. Use the coarse grinding plate, and allow the
meat to cure in a cool place for about 48 hours. Add
salt, in the same proportion, to the coarsely ground

pork the next evening and allow to cure overnight. (Some persons do not cure the pork.)

Regrind the cured beef, using the plate with 1/8-inch holes. Then add the pork and grind the mixture again. If the pork was not cured, add the salt (*13 ounces for 40 pounds of pork*) before grinding. Add spices and water and mix thoroughly until the mass is sticky. Thorough mixing often requires 30 minutes.

Tightly stuff the sausage into beef casings or muslin bags and allow it to hang and cure in a cool place overnight. Put it in a well-ventilated smokehouse heated to 110°F to 120°F. Protect the casings from a direct blaze that might scorch them. The sausage should take on a rich mahogany brown in about 2 hours' smoking.

Immediately put the hot, freshly smoked sausage into water heated to 160°F to 175°F, and cook it until it squeaks when the pressure of the thumb and finger on the casings is suddenly released. The usual cooking time for sausage stuffed in beef "rounds" is 15 to 30 minutes; for larger casings, 60 to 90 minutes. Plunge the cooked sausage into cold water to chill it. Hang it in a cool place.

From USDA Farmers' Bulletin No. 2138

BOLOGNA-STYLE SAUSAGE

In making bologna, for each 20 pounds of beef, add 5 pounds of fresh pork. Grind the meat coarse, then add the seasoning and grind through the fine plate.

For seasoning 25 pounds of meat, ½ pound of salt, and 2½ ounces of pepper are usually satisfactory. Garlic may be added if desired.

Add 3 or 4 pints of water to this quantity of meat. Mix with the hands until the water is entirely absorbed by the meat. When thoroughly mixed, stuff into soaked beef casings or "rounds," and smoke the bologna from 2 to 3 hours at a temperature of from 60°F to 70°F.

After smoking, cook the bologna in water about 200°F, or slightly below the boiling point, until it floats.

Keep the sausage in a dry place for immediate use, or can it by packing in cans, covering to within one-half inch of top with the liquid in which the bologna was cooked. Then heat it to a temperature of 250°F for 45 minutes, or at 15 pounds steam pressure.

From USDA Farmers' Bulletin No. 2209

ANDERSON FAMILY RECIPE
FOR SMOKED BEEF BOLOGNA

3 pounds of salt
2 pounds of sugar
6 teaspoons pepper (or more to taste)
3 ounces of saltpeter
100 pounds of beef ground as for hamburg

Mix well. Pack firmly into 3-inch diameter white muslin bags, any length from 1 to 2 feet, keeping out all air space (any air spaces will mold). Hang up and smoke at once until dark brown.

BLOOD SAUSAGE MADE WITH
MORTON TENDER-QUICK ®

It is easy to make good blood sausage.

3 gallons of hog's blood
7 lbs. beef hearts and trimmings
   (Beef trimmings may be used if enough hearts
   and tongues are not available)
2½ lbs. fat pork
½ lb. Tender-Quick®
1 oz. black pepper
Onions and mace may also be used

 To prepare the blood, stir it constantly while it is being collected until you have removed all the stringy fibres, leaving only the red liquid.

 Cook the beef and the pork together for about a half hour. Then remove from the fire and put the beef through a grinder, using plate with 1/8" holes.

 Cut the pork into small pieces and mix with the ground beef.

 Then stir in 4 oz. of Tender-Quick®, and stir the meat into the cold blood and add the remainder of the Tender-Quick® and seasoning ingredients.

 If this mixture is not thick enough for stuffing, add enough finely ground cornmeal to give it the consistency of thick mush. Stuff into beef casings and cook at a temperature of 160°F for 1½ hours or until a sharp pin can be run into the center (not through the sausage) and withdrawn without being followed by blood.

 Lay the sausages on a table for about ½ hour, turn them over and allow them to lie on the table another half hour. They will then be ready for use, but smoking for about 8 hours will improve their keeping qualities.

Source: "A Complete Guide to Home Meat Curing," published by the Morton Salt Company, Chicago, Illinois.

SUMMER SAUSAGE MADE WITH
MORTON TENDER-QUICK ® *

Summer sausage is a hard, dry sausage that is highly seasoned and will keep for a long time if stored in a dry place where it does not mold. A good summer sausage is made as follows:

> *20 lbs. lean beef*
> *10 lbs. lean pork*

Cut the pork into small pieces and store in layers not more than 6 inches in thickness for 20 days at 5°F. Remove the frozen pork from the freezer and allow to thaw. The beef is cut into small pieces and thoroughly mixed with the thawed pork. Then grind it once, using a plate with 3/16" holes. After the grinding, spread out the meat and add the following seasonings uniformly:

> *1 lb. Tender-Quick®*
> *2½ oz. finely ground black pepper*
> *2½ oz. sage*
> *1 oz. cane sugar*
> *½ oz. whole white pepper*
> *Garlic finely ground if desired*

Thoroughly mix the seasoning by kneading it into the meat, and regrind, using a plate with 1/8" holes, until the meat has been ground very fine. After the meat is seasoned and ground, spread it on wax paper in a cool, dry place for 3 or 4 days. Then stuff into casings and tie into 15 or 20" lengths. Rub the casings liberally with Sugar-Cure'™. Hang up and allow to dry and age for some time before using. Summer sausage may be smoked in a cool smoke if desired.

Source: "A Complete Guide to Home Meat Curing," published by the Morton Salt Company, Chicago, Illinois.

*See page 66 for information about Morton Tender-Quick.®

BLOOD SAUSAGE

As a basic starter, try the following recipe, remembering you are free to alter measurements to suit your taste or to add other spices and herbs as you prefer.

Cook five pounds of pork skin in 2 quarts of water.

Grind up 2 medium-sized onions and mix with the ground pork skin. Add salt, pepper, marjoram, ground cloves, and any other spices to suit your taste. Mix all thoroughly.

Now add 2 quarts of beef or pork blood, saved when the animals were slaughtered. Again, mix all together well.

Stuff the above mixture in casings and boil in plain water until the blood turns a dark-to-near-black color - usually about 15 - 20 minutes. Hang to dry, after which the stuffed casings may be smoked if desired before the sausages are later cooked for eating.

If no casings are available, mix everything well and boil; then pour into a pan to cool, cut into portions, and freeze.

INDEX

Ardennes ham (recipe) 181, 182

Bacteria,
  description 3
Beef 83-99
  aging 88
  bacon (recipe) 175
  broth for canning 91
  canning 88-95
    corned beef 94, 95
    cut up meat 91, 92
    ground meat 92, 93
    heart 95
    preparation of meat 90
    processing time, general, 91
    quantity of untrimmed meat
      needed per quart 30, 90
    sausage 93-94
    soup stock 95
    tongue 95
  chilling time before
    processing 45, 88
  corned beef (recipe) 173, 174
  curing 97-99
    preserving in lard 98
  dried beef (recipe) 168, 169
  freezing 96-97
    storage life 41, 97
  miscellaneous information 98, 99
  pickled beef (recipe) 187, 188
  pickled tripe (recipe) 184
  primary cuts 84-86
    diagram 85
  slaughtering 83, 84
  smoking
    pastrami (recipe) 187
  wasted meat 87, 88
  yield of dressed meat from
    carcass 87
Blood sausage (recipes) 194, 196
Bologna sausage (recipe) 191-193
Botulism 3, 4 (see also Spoilage)

Brine cure (see Curing meat, brine.
    See also under specific meats.)
Buffalo, where to obtain 138
Butcher's wrap 46; illus. 48-49

Can(s)
  advantages of, 29
  description of, 22
  packing 30-34
    hot pack 33
    raw pack 33
  preparation for canning 22
    (see also Jars)
Can and jar lifter 17; illus. 18
"Can or freez" jars 28, 44, 46
Canning 11-37
  advantages of, 11-12
  cans 22
    advantages of, 29
  cooling 35
  definition 13
  equipment 14-17, 22-29; illus. 15,
    17, 18, 23, 24-27
  expelling air 31, 32
  jars 23-29; illus. 23-27
    advantages of, 29
    hints for using 27, 28
  labeling 36
  meat selection 12, 13
  methods 8, 20
    oven 8
    steam pressure 21
    water bath 20
  packing jars or cans
    hints 33
    hot pack 33
    raw pack 33
  pressure canner 14-16; illus. 15
  processing cans and jars 34
  quantity of untrimmed meat
    needed per quart 30, 90, 106,
    131

Canning (continued)
  reason for heat 14
  sealer for cans 16
  sealing containers 34
  storage 36
  (see also specific meats)
Casings 116, 117
Chicken (see Poultry)
Clams (see Fish, shellfish)
Corn cobs, use in smoking 80
Corned beef
  canning 94, 95
  recipes 173, 174
Country ham (recipe) 178, 179
Crab (see Fish, shellfish)
Curing 53-72
  brine 59-62
    definition 54
    pumping 61, 62, 134; illus. 62, 63
    standard recipe 59
  definition 53
  dry cure 56-58
    definition 54
    standard recipe for, 57, 58
  drying 63
  equipment 56; illus. 57
  hints 71, 72
  insects, protecting meat from,
    66-70; illus. 67
  overhauling 58, 60
  preparation of meat 55
  prepared curing products 65, 66
  storage 63, 64, 68, 69;
    illus. 65, 70, 72
  sweet pickle (see Curing, brine)
  wrapping 63, 64; illus. 64
  (see also specific meats)

Drugstore fold 46; illus. 47
Dry cure (see Curing, dry cure. See
  also under specific meats.)
Drying meat
  dried beef (recipe) 168, 169
Duck (see Poultry)

Enzymes, description 2
Expelling air (see under Canning)

Fast freezing 40, 49, 50
Field dressing (see Game, field
  dressing)
Fire pit 74; illus. 75
Fish 147-165
  air drying 165
  canning 155-160
    fish chowder (recipe) 183
  chilling time before
    processing 45, 150
  care of before processing 147
  curing 161-163
    brine 162, 163
      storage time 163
    dry curing 161, 162
  fin fish
    canning 155-158
      river herring 157
      roe 158
      salmon and shad 156
      salt water fish 157
  fillet, how to 149
  freezing 150-153
    brine for freezing 152
    glazing 152
    preparation for freezing;
      illus. 151
    roe 152
    storage life 41, 153
    yield 152
  preparation for processing
    148-149
  fish chowder (recipe) 183
  general 147
  pickled fish (recipe) 184
  pickling 165
  shellfish
    canning 159-160
      clams 159
      crab meat 159
      shrimp 160
    freezing 154
      storage life 154
    pickled oysters (recipe) 186
  smoking 163-165
    preparation for processing 149-150
Fowl 145-146
  canning 145

Fowl (continued)
    freezing 145
    storage life 146
    smoking 146
Freezer burn 39
Freezer paper 44
Freezers
    chest type 40, 52
    upright 40, 52
Freezing 39-52
    advantages and disadvantages of,
        41, 42
    chilling time before freezing 45
    cured meats 71
    definition 39
    equipment 43, 44
    kinds of meat to freeze 43
    labeling 48, 49
    power failure 50
    preparation of meat 45
    refreezing meat 51
    storage life 41, 97
    summary 51, 52
    temperature 40
    thawing 51
        wrapping 39, 46; illus. 47
    (see also specific meats)

Game 137-146
    chilling time before processing
        45, 141
    field dressing 139, 141, 143, 144;
        illus. 140, 143
    health of, 141
    large game animals 142
        canning 142
        curing and smoking 142
        freezing 142
    preparation for processing 138, 139
    safety precautions 141
    small game animals 143-145
        canning 144
        curing and smoking 144, 145
        freezing 144
            storage life 144
    venison mincemeat (recipe) 172
Giblets (see Poultry)
Goose (see Poultry)

Grades of meat
    Canada 7
    U.S. 6, 7
        federal grading stamp, illus. 6,
Ground meat
    freezing, storage life 41

Ham (see Pork, smoking; also under
    Recipes)
Headroom, definition 32
Headspace (see Headroom)
Herring (see Fish, fin fish)

Information on meat processing,
    sources of, 9
Insects, protecting meat from, (see
    under Curing)
Inspection of meat
    Canadian government 5; stamp
        illus. 5
    U.S. government 4, 5, 6, 125;
        stamp illus. 4, 5, 125

Jars
    advantages of, 29
    description 23-29; illus. 23-27
    for freezing 28
    hints for using 27, 28
    packing 30-34
        hot pack 33
        raw pack 33
    preparation 28
    selection 27, 28
    (see also Can(s))
Jerky (recipe) 170

Labeling 36, 48, 49, 153
Lake trout (see Fish, fin fish)
Lamb 119-24
    canning 121
    chilling time before processing 45, 119
    curing 122, 123
        brine cure 123
        dry cure 122, 123
    freezing 121
        storage life 41, 122

‹s 119
‹21; illus. 120

‹ed meat from
‹121

‹g in 98
‹t (recipe) 190
‹see Fish, shellfish)

‹erel (see Fish, fin fish)
‹ple sugar pickle for ham (recipe)
    180
Mincemeat (recipe) 172
Molds (microorganisms),
    description 3
Mullet (see Fish, fin fish)

Organ meat
    freezing, storage life 41
Overhauling 58, 60
Oyster (see Fish, shellfish)

Pemmican (recipe) 171
Pennsylvania Dutch ham (recipe) 178
Pork 101-112
    Ardennes ham (recipe) 181, 182
    bacon (recipe) 175; (see also
        Ardennes ham)
    Canadian bacon (recipe) 175
    canning 105, 106
        suitability of various cuts 105
        quantity of untrimmed meat
            needed per quart 106
    chilling time before
        processing 45, 101
    curing 106-110
        brine 109, 110
            general recipe 109
            storage of meat 110
        dry curing 107-109
            general recipe 107-109
            general 106-107
            sweet pickle cure (see Pork,
                curing, brine)

Pork (continued)
    fat, uses for, 111, 112
    freezing 106
        storage life, 41, 106
    ham (recipes) 176-182
    lard 111
    maple sugar pickle for ham
        (recipe) 180
    pickled pork (recipe) 187
    preparation of carcass 101
    primary cuts 102-104; diagram 103
    salt pork 112
    smoking 110-111
        loss of weight 111
        Smithfield hams 111
        storage 111
        yield of dressed meat from
            from carcass 104, 105
Poultry 125-135
    broth for canning 128
    canning 128-131
        giblets 131
        hot pack 128, 129
            with bone 128
            without bone 129
        quantity of untrimmed meat
            needed per quart 131
        raw pack 129, 130
            with bone 129
            without bone 130
    chilling time before processing
        45, 132
    curing and smoking 133
        choice of meat for, 133
        storage 135
    cutting up 126, 127; illus, 127
    freezing 131-133
        storage life 41, 133
    general 125
    inspection and grading 125
        federal stamps, illus. 125, 126
Power failure (see Freezing, power
    failure)
Pressure canner
    adjustment for high altitudes 16
    care of 16
    general 14, 34; illus. 15
    necessity 14

Pressure canner (continued)
  selection 14
Pressure cooker for canning 14
Processing of meat, definition 1
Pumping 61, 62, 134; illus. 62, 63

Recipes 167-196
  Ardennes ham 181, 182
  bacon 175 (see also Ardennes ham)
  bacon, beef 175
  bacon, Canadian 175
  beef (see Ardennes ham)
  blood sausage 194, 196
  bologna sausage 191, 192, 193
  corned beef 173, 174
  country ham 178, 179
  cured tongue 174
  dried beef 168, 169
  fish chowder 183
  general 167-168
  ham 176, 182
  ham, Pennsylvania Dutch style 178
  jerky 170
  liver sausage, Pennsylvania Dutch
    style 190, 191
  liverwurst 190
  maple sugar pickle for ham 180
  mincemeat, venison 172
  pastrami 187
  pemmican 171
  Pennsylvania Dutch-style ham
    178
  pickled beef and pork 187, 188
  pickled fish 184, 185
  pickled oysters 186
  pickled tripe 184
  sausages 188-196
  smoked beef bologna 193
  smoked sausage 189
  summer sausage 195, 196
  tongue 174
  trout (see Ardennes ham)
  turkey (see Ardennes ham)
  venison (see Ardennes ham)
  venison mincemeat 172

Safety in processing meat 7, 18-20,
  44, 45

Salmon (see Fish, fin fish)
Saltpeter, controversy over, 54
Sanitary precautions
  necessity when canning 19, 20
  necessity when curing 55
  necessity when freezing 44, 45
Sausage 113-118, 188-196
  casings 116, 117
  fat, proportion to lean 113
  freezing
    storage life 41
  general information 113, 115
  general recipe 118
  recipes 188-196
  storage 115, 116
  taste testing recipe 117
Sausage grinders 114-115
Scallops (see Fish, shellfish)
Sealer for cans 16
Shad (see Fish, fin fish)
Shrimp (see Fish, shellfish)
Smoke chamber 74-77; illus. 75, 76
Smoke tunnel 77-79; illus. 75, 77, 78
Smokehouse 73-82
  how to build 74-82; illus. 75, 76, 77,
    78, 82
  important considerations 79
  source of additional information 82
Smoking 70, 71, 73, 80, 81
  cold smoking, definition 72
  fire 79, 80
  fuel 80-81
    where to obtain 81
  general 70, 71
  hot smoking, definition 72
Soap 111
Spoilage
  signs of 20, 36
  test for 20, 36
Storage of meats
  length of time frozen 41
  temperature for cured meats 70

Temperature
  aging 88, 101, 119, 142, 145
  canning 14, 19, 28, 31, 73, 91-95,
    128-131, 156-160
  hot pack 19, 31, 92, 93, 128, 129

')
...sing 45, 55,
..., 150
...07, 108, 109,

...es 2, 19, 31, 32
...oorganisms 2, 19, 31, 32
...r in canning 31
...ing 40, 49, 51
...temperature chart (illus.)

...age of cured meat 70, 98, 111,
162, 163
...torage of frozen meat 40, 50, 51,
101, 122, 133, 153, 154
Thermometer for meat caning 17, 32
Tongue
curing 174
Trichinosis 39, 101, 102, 141
Tripe, pickled (recipe) 184

U.S. Department of Agriculture,
address of, 9

Veal 99-100
chilling time before
processing 45, 99
freezing 100
storage life 41, 100
preparation of meat for
processing 99

Whitefish (see Fish, fin fish)
Wrapping 39, 46-48, 63-65, 91, 111,
124, 132, 133, 152-154, 164, 165;
illus. 47, 64, 65

Yeasts, description 3